Endangered

and Endemic Birds

of The Dominican Republic

Endangered and Endemic Birds of The Dominican Republic

Annabelle Stockton Dod

Cypress House
Fort Bragg, CA 95437

Library of Congress Cataloging-in-Publications Data

Dod, Annabelle S.

Endangered and endemic birds of the Dominican Republic / Annabelle S. Dod. — 1st ed.

p.   cm.

ISBN 1-879384-12-4 (pbk.) : $12.00

1. Birds—Dominican Republic. I. Title

QL688.D6D63   1992

598.297293—dc20   91-76656

CIP

r92

Printed in the U.S.A.

CREDITS

The illustrations for this book have been given to me personally over a period of several years. They were contributed by the following people: Jose Alberto Ottenwalder, James Wiley, Angus Nader, Jose Ramon Osorio, Segundo Reyes, David Shibly, Francisco Rivas, George B. Reynard, and my husband, Donald D. Dod.

"The Black Rail *(Laterallus Jamaicensis)* in Hispaniola" scientific report is reprinted with permission from *American Birds*.

"He Sings His Own Name in Spanish: The Least Pauraque" is reprinted with permission from *American Birds*.

"A New Race of Chat Tanager *(Calyptophilus frugivorus)* from the Dominican Republic" is reprinted with permission from *Notulae Naturae*, the Academy of Natural Sciences of Philadelphia.

"An Ornithologist Can See More than Birds: A Curiosity of Hispaniola" is reprinted by permission from *Defenders* magazine. Copyright © 1980 by Defenders of Wildlife.

Dedication

This book is dedicated to Mrs. Jean Heflin, who inspired me to write it.

Dr. George B. Reynard

Acknowledgments

I wish to express my gratitude to all my friends who live in the *campos* of the Dominican Republic. They have always been willing to help the Bird Woman, being patient with my Spanglish, often sharing their food and shelter, and willingly giving assistance when our temperamental Volkswagen minibus went on the blink or when we got stuck in the mud.

The members of the Armed Forces, the Department of Wild Life, the National Park Office, and my colleagues at the Museo Nacional de Historia Natural (National Museum of Natural History) have been most helpful.

Mrs. Jean Heflin of the CODETEL (telephone company) deserves special recognition. Busy lady as she was, she gave freely of her time and knowledge to help translate and type my Spanish articles into English. To her I owe my most profound gratitude.

I am also grateful to José Alberto Ottenwalder, Roy Brogan, Bruce Sorrie, Arthur Plowman and Kathy Luke for their help in the in the field of photography. Also my thanks to my husband, Donald D. Dod, who has been a willing worker in this field and who is responsible for the greater part of the photography in this book.

Dr. George Reynard of Riverton, New Jersey, has been a great and loyal friend, who often accompanied us on our travels through the Dominican Republic. George was the official recorder for our team, making tapes of the vocalizations, which were later made into a record called "Bird Songs from the Dominican Republic."

I would be remiss if I did not mention James Bond, author of the book, *Birds of the West Indies*. By being a faithful and informative correspondent, he gave me encouragement and support. To Robert Arbib, retired editor of *American Birds*, I am deeply indebted. He not only edited the manuscript, he helped me learn the details of publishing.

To them all I give my hearty "Muchas Gracias" for their companionship, their cooperation and the many pleasant memories I have of our almost 20 years of gathering material for this book.

Annabelle Stockton Dod

Table of Contents

1   Foreword

3   Introduction

7   The Origin of the Species

15 The Devil's Nesting Place: The Black-capped Petrel

25 The Industrious Canopy Fisher: The Reddish Egret

30 An Endangered Species: The West Indian Whistling Duck

33 A Seldom-seen Duck: The White-cheeked Pintail

36 A Helpful, Endangered Friend: The Ridgway's Hawk

42 A Prediction Fulfilled: The Spotted Rail

46 A Bird that Lives in the Habitat of a Rat: The Black Rail

51 Adios, Beautiful: The White-crowned Pigeon

57 The Bird with the Foghorn Voice: The Gray-headed Quail Dove

61 Polly Parrot Becomes Cuca, La Cotorra: The Hispaniolan Parrot

65 The Termite Nest is Home to the Parakeet: The Hispaniolan Parakeet

68 A Very Deceitful Bird: The Bay-breasted Cuckoo

75 The Cuckoo That Isn't Crazy: The Hispaniolan Lizard Cuckoo

80 A Devil in Bird's Feathers: The Stygian Owl

85 A Witch That Flies On Wings, Not a Broomstick: The Potoo

89 He Sings His Own Name in Spanish: The Least Pauraque

93 A Living Jewel: The Emerald Hummingbird

96 He Flirts His Metallic Tail: The Mango Hummingbird

103 A Mighty Mite: The Vervain Hummingbird

106 A Barking Dog with Geranium-red Underparts: The Hispaniolan Trogan

109 The Deceptive Little Green Todies:Broad and Narrow-billed Todies

113 The Little Bird With the Big Voice: The Hispaniolan Piculet

117 Friend or Foe?: The Hispaniolan Woodpecker

120 An Overlooked Flycatcher: The Greater Antillean Elaenia

124 When Green Turns to Gold: The Golden Swallow

130 A Crow is a Crow in Any Language: The White-necked Crow

135 A Messenger from Eden: The La Selle's Thrush

139 A Very Endemic Bird: The Palm Chat

145 The Ghost Singer: The Rufous-throated Solitaire

149 A Very Different Vireo: The Flat-billed Vireo

157 A Shady Character from the Forest Floor: The Ground Warbler

160 The Warbler That Turned Into a Tanager: The White-winged Warbler

165 The Bright, Dark Queen of the Forest: The Stripe-headed Tanager

168 A Resourceful, Common Tanager: The Black-crowned Palm Tanager

171 The Problem Birds from the Island of Hispaniola: The Chat Tanagers

178 The Clown of the Show: The Hispaniolan Siskin

181 The White-winged Crossbill is Now Considered Endemic

185 A Finch That Can Pinch: The Greater Antillean Bullfinch

188 A Misplaced Sparrow: The Rufous-collared Sparrow

192 An Ornithologist Sees More Than Birds: A Curiosity of Hispaniola

199 Glossary

201 List of Birds of the Dominican Republic

Endangered

and Endemic Birds

of The Dominican Republic

Foreword

The birds in the Dominican Republic are part of the culture and beliefs of the Dominican people. Ever since the Arawak Indians lived on this island, birds have been part of people's spiritual lives—in tales and myths—and also of their everyday meals. Today this continues, both the myth and the food. We still see youngsters forming groups to hunt for birds, mainly the Cigua *(Dulus dominicus)* to make "locrios de cigua." This heritage, this tradition, has created a deep interest among Dominicans in their birds. It is hard to find a person in the Dominican Republic who cannot tell you a story about birds in his life.

Mrs. Dod has gathered in this book the tales and myths about birds of the Dominican Republic, compiling a cultural treasure from several generations in some cases and in others, the experiences of one man or family.

It is important to note tales such as the ones about the Ciguapa, the Pitanguá, and the La Selle's Thrush or Cho-Chó. These are birds that Mrs. Dod worked very hard to find. In the case of the Ciguapa (Stygian Owl), she clearly establishes, finally, that this is a bird and not a supernatural being as was long believed in the Dominican Republic.

For her contribution to scientific knowledge about birds, cultural values, and the life experiences of the Dominican people, Mrs. Dod is now considered a Dominican—not only by her close friends but also by the many Dominicans who read every Saturday her newspaper column about nature in the Dominican Republic.

Francisco X. Geraldes, *Director*

National Museum of Natural History

Santo Domingo

1

Introduction

Naturalists began observations on the island that Columbus called Hispaniola with his very first voyage. In August, 1493, when the Great Explorer made his triumphant return to Spain, he carried with him several live parrots and parakeets as well as bird skins, to show and impress the Queen who had sponsored his explorations. There were also verbal reports of birds seen and heard but not captured. One enthusiastic account mentioned a bird that sang like a nightingale, which is taken to have been the mockingbird, since that species has always been considered common on this island.

From subsequent voyages, men told tales of killing pigeons with sticks so as to have fresh meat. Sea birds were reported in great numbers; they were hunted during nesting season, the eggs being robbed and used as food.

According to reports, study in the discipline of ornithology was very incidental. The first real work of describing the various species did not begin until 1523. By 1557, Fernando de Oviedo y Valdez, who made 12 voyages across the Atlantic, finally wrote up 11 species. The descriptions were credible until he described a monstruous bird from Puerto Rico and Hispaniola that had one foot like that of a duck and the other like that of an eagle. It ate both fish and fowl with indifference!

Very little ornithological work was done by the later explorers of the 15th century. In 1618 Rochefort wrote about the flamingos, pigeons, and parrots. However, he was not interested in them for scentific study but for hunting and sport. In 1700 Father Labot wrote about the thrushes and parakeets. In 1760 Brisson described and published 33 species. In 1788 Chervain used acceptable scientific names, which made his work important.

3

During the French colonial period, much work was done in natural history in Haiti, but the explorers did not go beyond the border as they were at odds with Spain. Naturalists came from Sweden, Germany, France, England, and the United States of America. Each explorer wrote his accounts of the investigations in his own native language, and of course the reports seldom if ever reached the institutions of learning in Hispaniola.

It was not until after 1844 when the Dominican Republic gained its independence from Haiti that a semblance of political stability came to the country. In 1849 the era of exploration began. During the next 78 years, work was done mostly by North Americans, with the Academy of Natural Sciences in Philadelphia and the Smithsonian Institution of Washington D.C. taking the lead. But the reports were all in English, and the material collected went to enrich the museums of the North.

Charles B. Cory was one of the outstanding ornithologists of his time. He worked in the Dominican Republic and Haiti from 1881 to 1883. A book was published in four parts, beginning in March 1884 and completed a year later. One hundred and eleven species were described, and many forms were illustrated in color paintings.

In June and July, 1883, Dr. W. L. Abbott began his work in the Dominican Republic, starting his collection on the peninsula of Samaná. After his first visit there came a long list of ornithologists, but his reports and those of another indefatigable explorer, Rollo H. Beck, were the most detailed and usable. Of course all these accounts were written in English, with only one person—Rafael Ciferri, an Italian working for the Dominican government in the Agricultural School in Moca—writing in Spanish. He made annual reports for the department but it seems that no one knows what became of the published material.

When Dr. Abbott returned to the island in 1916, he worked with few interruptions from that year until 1923. His work and his reports led to the writing of Bulletin #155, "Birds of Haiti and the Dominican Republic," by Alexander Wetmore and Bradshaw H. Swales, which was published in 1931. This book made a great contribution to the scientific knowledge of the avifauna of Hispaniola. In addition to the descriptions of the birds, a detailed ornithological history of the island was given.

James Bond, curator of birds at the Academy of Natural Sciences in Philadelphia, wrote "A Field Guide to the Birds of the West Indies." This important work was first published in 1936, and since then four more editions have been printed. However, the work of both Bond and Abbott was limited in time and scope. Both explorers collected specimens in the peninsula of Samaná and the Cordillera Central. They both worked extensively in Haiti, in the Massif de la Selle and the Massif de la Hotte, which are extensions of the Baoruco range in the Dominican Republic.

By 1931 the avifauna of Hispaniola were fairly well-known by scientists outside the island, but the Dominican people knew very little of their own birds. The language barrier was not the only reason for this situation. Political repression, superstitious fear of the unknown, the heavily wooded and inaccessible wild mountains, the stories of nomadic runaway slaves, and the inclement weather all made exploration very difficult. Although biology, zoology, herpetology and anthropology have been included in the curricula of the universities for many years, there has never been a course offered in ornithology.

It is no wonder that the people are still ignorant about the birds, no wonder that they are superstitious about them, no wonder there has been uncontrolled hunting and wholesale destruction of habitat by fire and the cutting of forests.

But conditions are slowly changing. We have an organized Ornithological Society. Two comparatively new governmental institutions have been created, the National Museum of Natural History and a Department of Wild Life. We have a record of bird songs from the Dominican Republic. We have some students who are interested in ornithological careers. We have regular Christmas Bird Counts as a community activity.

We have great hopes for a responsible conservation program that will soon be nationwide. If that happens perhaps you, too, will be able to enjoy some of our beautiful birds on the island of Hispaniola.

At present 225 species are known in the Dominican Republic. There are 131 nesting species, 22 of which are endemic and 11 are introduced. The remainder are winter residents and transitory species.

Haiti has two known residents that do not live in the Dominican Republic. The Gray-crowned Palm Tanager *(Phaenicophilus pollocephalus)* is endemic to the southern peninsula of Haiti. The Tawny- shouldered Blackbird *(Agelaius humeralis)* in Haiti is known only from the lower Artibonite River and from the vicinity of Port-de-Paix.

The Origin of the Species

My husband, Donald D. Dod, and I arrived in the Dominican Republic from our home in Puerto Rico in the fall of 1964. We had been invited there by the Evangelical Church to work in a special program of social action. The country was more than ready for social reform. After 30 years of tyrannical rule by a hard-line dictator, followed by several political upheavals and finally an open civil war, there were many problems to be solved. Nearly 85% of the land remained in the hands of 5% of the people. Less than 65% of the people were literate, and there was a population explosion as well as a high death rate. (Life expectancy stood at 52 years.) Malnourishment and all the ills that go with it were widespread on a national scale. Since we had been working for 18 years in these fields in a Third World situation in Puerto Rico, the Church Council in the Dominican Republic wanted us to start working in Family Planning, as this was the area where they saw the greatest need. The entire country would be our field of endeavor.

Don and I have been naturalists almost all our lives, and the idea of exploring new areas where there were still virgin forests, high mountains and white water rivers appealed to us. We arranged our work so we could have 3 days in the office in the capital, two days in the villages, and weekends to study the birds and the orchids.

We started to work immediately in the capital. By February, 1965, we were well organized and ready to work in the interior, which led us far afield and into the boondocks.

It became evident early on that we had walked into a vacuum. Trujillo had sponsored programs to promote the large family concept. He paid bounties and promoted contests to see who could have the most offspring. He allowed no information about family planning to come into the country and for a time he did not allow

7

the doctors to go off the island to study. As a result, there was much to be done.

We had some exciting times working with the country people. Each village had its own customs and beliefs, fears and foibles, making each visit a story in itself. It did not take us long to discover that the love of wild life and its conservation were completely new ideas to people who had to eke out a living in the mountains. It seemed that everything was their enemy, and that their life-style was built on the premise that you had to defend yourself. If a tree was green, it was to be chopped down. If it was dry, it had to be burned. If something moved, it had to be killed.

As a result of this philosophy, we have seen horrendous destruction. Virgin forests have been chopped and burned in one place after another. The ground would be cleared for planting and used for two years, then the people would move on to "clean" more land. Watersheds have been denuded and rivers have dried up. Birds of every species were killed for sport and many used for food. No one seemed to recognize this as a problem nor was anyone willing to do anything about it. What could two foreigners do in the face of such conditions? I decided I would launch a program of environmental education of my own.

I visited our friend, Doña María Ugarte, who edited the Saturday supplement for *El Caribe*, one of the largest daily newspapers. With her approval and help, I started a weekly column that spoke out against the wanton destruction of the birds and their habitats, and advocated measures for their conservation. Doña María edited my Spanish articles and published every one.

About this time we received help and inspiration from an unexpected source. In 1968 we met Dr. George B. Reynard, a plant geneticist and naturalist whose hobby of recording bird songs took him into the hills at every opportunity. He made regular trips to the Dominican Republic to supervise the winter tomato crops for Campbell Soup Company. He was our companion on many of our weekend trips. We were highly organized. George was chief recorder and visiting ornithologist. He helped us with difficult identifications of the wintering species with which we had had little or no acquaintance. He was also the night watchman. He slept on a cot under a mosquito net, protected only by a plastic roof. This gave him a better opportunity to hear night birds and to be out and ready to record at a minute's notice. Don served as chauffeur, photographer, handyman, collector, botanist. I was the ornithologist, coordinator, chief cook and bottle washer, tender of the mist nets, curator of birds, and the silent member of the trio that sang on the way home. Each one of us kept our own field notes.

After Don and I had been doing investigative work in the country for some time, we were asked to participate in a cultural program initiated by the government. Don was asked to work as Curator of Birds and Orchids in the National Botanical Gardens, and to be in charge of the ecological aspect of the grounds. A little later I was asked to be in charge of the Ornithological Section in the National Museum of Natural History. We both decided these would be wonderful opportunities to further the cause of conservation and we accepted our positions with great anticipation. We turned our family planning work over to the Public Health Department and the Family Planning Association, then went to work full-time as naturalists and conservationists.

We have had some memorable experiences. I was arrested twice. The first time I was arrested (see story on page 75) it was aggravating and inconvenient but of no consequence. The second time was scary and had repercussions. My husband had gone down the creek bed to look for orchids, so I was left alone to tend the mist nets. We were camped in a good spot near an irrigation project so there were many birds flying about. I was very busy and was not paying any attention to anything around me. Suddenly I was grabbed from behind, my arms pinned down to my sides and then a pistol was jabbed into my ribs. My documents were demanded and under protest I was taken to the police station.

After reviewing my passport, my identification card and reading the letter of permission to do scientific studies, signed by Dr. Joaquin Balaguer, the President of the country, the Chief of Police decided that I was harmless. "But," he said, "the next time you come to stay all night, you should check in at the Station. The neighbors reported you people as suspicious-looking characters. They think you are communists."

We reported several times. After awhile they told us that we didn't need to report any more.

We went through some wild storms with gale winds, lightning and thunder, and flash floods. We were hungry the day our food ran out after a wild burro or pig raided our food sacks. I caught the flu from over-exposure; we both have had diarrhea from drinking polluted water and at various times we have harbored several kinds of intestinal parasites. We have had rashes and skin allergies from contact with poisonous plants. We have been bitten by mosquitoes, wasps, fleas, no-see-ums, ants and bedbugs. We have escaped the centipedes and hairy spiders, but twice Don was stung by scorpions.

We have experienced both extreme heat and cold. There are large expanses of desert with no water and very little shade. The tropical sun can beat you down if you stay out in it too long. The cold can be just as bad. Some of our lofty mountains reach upward to 10,000 feet. (Pico Duarte and Pico Pelona are the two highest points in all the West Indies) and to those people who are used to a warm climate, the cold can be a terrible shock if adequate preparations are not made.

Our most enjoyable times have been with people. As the *campesinos* became used to our coming and going, we gained their confidence. They called me the "Bird Woman," Don was "The Plant Man," and George was "El Blanco."

We rigged our Volkswagen bus with a small propane stove, a bed and a folding table. We cooked, ate, and slept in the car, and then when we wanted to move, our whole house went with us! People would gather around to see how it was done. The conversations that ensued gave us the opportunity to offer information on Family Planning, nutrition, and intestinal parasites. (We always carried medicine along with us, and often gave it out.) We also talked about the waste of burning and some agricultural practices that are outdated. We gave lectures on conserving our natural resources.

Sometimes our conversations would lead to lengthy discussions on politics, religion, history and philosophy, beliefs and superstitions. We learned about the "Gente Pequeña" (Little People), the "Bacá" (the Devil), the "Dun-dunes" (Mischievous Dwarfs), and the "Bruja" (the Witch). But the most common subject of all was the "Ciguapa."

The Ciguapa is a creature believed to live in the primitive forests and remote areas. It is supposed to come out at night to perform acts of depredation, like stealing food from the plantations or running off with a handsome young man. It has the form of a woman about three feet tall, with long, flowing hair that hangs down to the knees. The feet are fastened on backwards and for that reason it is very difficult to catch one. Only a completely black male dog with a fifth toe is capable of tracking and capturing a Ciguapa.

People marvelled that we did not carry a gun to protect ourselves from the Ciguapa. They would ask us if we were afraid, and if we said we were not, they would think we did not believe in its existence. We learned never to deny its existence, but to say we thought the Ciguapa was probably extinct, since we had never seen one.

But no matter if our opinions were different, no matter if our customs and life-styles were beyond comprehension, the *campesinos* were always friendly and they were always there, ready to help us if we needed them.

We were stuck in the mud several times. And once our rear right wheel fell into a deep hole. We tried in vain to get out, and I am sure we would be sitting there still if a group of agricultural workers had not come by. They literally picked up our heavily loaded bus and placed it "beside" the hole.

The funniest thing that ever happened to us was when George and a cane-cutter scared each other. Early one morning, about 4:30 a.m., George heard the loud "Hoo" of the Stygian Owl. He managed to crawl out from under his mosquito net and put on all his recording paraphernalia without mishap. He started off down the trail to a large tree at the turn in the road. As he rounded the curve he unexpectedly met a man. They had taken each other by surprise, so they both called out. With his machete in hand, the cane-cutter ventured a little closer, took one look, gave another yelp and ran full tilt down the road. George came back to the car a bit shaken. He could not understand why the poor man had been so afraid.

"Look at yourself, George," said my husband. "The man thought you were from another planet!"

And George did look the part. His earphones and antenna made his head look like that of a huge bug. The recorder on the shoulder-strap, the microphone around his neck, and the big parabola made a complete outfit. He looked like a well-dressed man from Mars!

By 1976 my nature column in *El Caribe* was a decided success. It had been running for five years, and I had written enough articles about the birds, the loss of their habitats, the cause and effect of deforestation, folklore, social conditions, and the need for conservation to fill a large book. People were reading my column and collecting my stories. I had telephone calls, fan mail, and invitations to visit special environments. I gave slide-shows at primary schools. I was asked to give lectures to clubs, societies, and biology classes in secondary schools as well as the university. I even performed for social functions and was invited to the American Embassy on two occasions. I appeared on television several times. An Ornithological Society was organized and I was asked to make a compilation of my articles to be published in book form. I did not have to be asked twice. I thought this would be an excellent way to publicize the need for governmental action and cooperation in the conservation of our natural resources.

I began work at once. I had line-drawing illustrations made for each species. I made maps showing exactly where each species is to be found. We had 114 color illustrations, 22 of endemic species and the remainder of rare or hard-to-identify species. By 1977 the book was finished and in 1978 the Museo Nacional del Historia Natural published it as *Aves de la República Dominica (Birds of the Dominican Republic)*. For the first time in history, the Dominican people had a book written in Spanish that they could read and from it learn about some of the wonderful things in their own country. The book turned out to be a best-seller. It is certified by the Department of Education as a resource book for teachers at all levels, and is now out of print.

In 1981 I wrote a field guide to the birds of the Dominican Republic in Spanish and two coloring books for children. We finished the recording of bird songs. These were presented to the public in a ceremony under the auspices of the National Parks. After this activity we began to get attention from the government and its institutions. The year 1984 was named the Year of Conservation.

When our accomplishments are summed up, they look like a lot of work and they were. But it was enjoyable for people nearing retirement age who could and would make a contribution to the scientific knowledge of the country. My husband has found over 115 orchids new to the country, about 100 of them new to science and endemic to the island of Hispaniola. I have found two birds new to science, two new resident species, four introduced birds that have become established, and many migrant birds never before listed. We have found the nests of six species that had never before been seen by scientists on the Island of Hispaniola.

There are still many interesting areas to be explored. Although we still go out as consultants and guides, our efforts are now mostly in the field of education. That, too, is enjoyable work, but the hills are my home and they still have the same fascination for me as they did years ago in northern California. I can only wish I were 40 years younger!

The stories in this book are elaborated English versions of the ones that were written first in Spanish for the people of the Dominican Republic. Because much of our avifauna is the same as the species of North and Central America, I chose to write about the endemic species and some of the rare ones that are on their way to extinction.

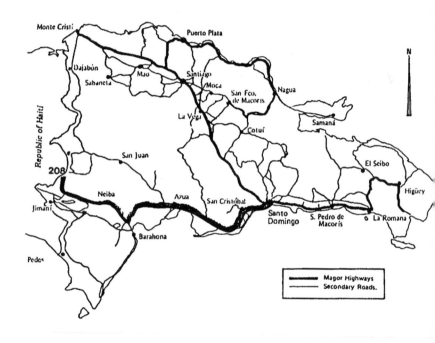

The Dominican Republic

The Devil's Nesting Place

The Black-capped Petrel

Order: Procellariiformes
Family: Procellariidae
Scientific name: *Pterodroma hasitata*
English name: Black-capped Petrel
Spanish name: Diablotín

The Black-capped Petrel belongs to a strange, pelagic family of birds called *Procellariidae* or the Tube Noses. They are so called because the air for the lungs is carried back in paired tubes along the ridge of the bill to the nostril. The bill is hooked, equipped to eat any kind of food: live fish, dead animals, or decomposed materials. The feet are webbed, and the legs short and weak. The wings are pointed and comparatively long, giving them great power of flight. The birds are about the size of a large pigeon.

Little was known in the Dominican Republic about this species as it was seldom seen near land, and when the age of exploration began it was already in decline.

According to the historical record, the Black-capped Petrel *(Pterodroma hasitata)* was first described by Buffon in 1783 *(Natural History,* Vol. 9). It was reported from Haiti or Saint Domingue, as the island was then called; therefore there is no way of telling in what part of the island it was actually found. Only four reports from the Dominican Republic are known. They are as follows: E.E. Richmond observed three Diablotines flying toward land on the north coast in April, 1900. E. Moltoni reported that a bird of this species was captured in Moca by R. Ciferri on May 10, 1928. Alexander Wetmore and J.T. Nichols reported seeing 100 in the Caribbean area in 1931, and four of them were collected.Then there was a lapse of 48 years before any other reports were made.

In August, 1977, José Alberto Ottenwalder and James Wiley observed the Black-capped Petrel in the waters around Beata, a small island off the south coast of Santo Domingo. On June 3, 1977, a dead juvenile of this species was found at the edge of the Laguna de Rincón at Cabral. More recently another juvenile was taken alive on August 15, 1984. This specimen, in a very weakened condition, was turned over to a caretaker in the National Zoological Park in Santo Domingo. Even though it was offered small pieces of sardines, it refused to eat, and before morning it was dead. There was no data as to where the bird had been found; the man who turned it over to the caretaker said someone had given the bird to him.

My attention was first called to the Black-capped Petrel during a visit to the Sierra de Baoruco in October, 1971. Dr. Cameron Kepler and his wife, Dr. Angela Kepler, ornithologists from Puerto Rico, accompanied my husband and me on an investigative expedition to Zapotén, on the border between the Dominican Republic and Haiti.

Because the condition of the road would not permit travel by car beyond the Zapotén area at a 1550-meter elevation we made camp on the flat where a sawmill had once been installed. This particular locality is a delightful mixture of environments. Within an area of one square mile, there were deep, dark canyons, beautiful alpine meadows, broadleaf forests, pine forests, and virgin jungles. The proximity of the large inland salt lake, Lago Enriquillo, at below sea level added to the possibility of seeing rare species. It was, in truth, a bird-watcher's paradise.

We saw our first La Selle's Thrush in Zapotén, and there we had our first glimpse of the Chat tanager. We found a nest of the Pitangúa, the Greater Antillean Night Jar, and of the White-winged Crossbill. There we caught a White-winged Warbler in our net, and held the famous Rufous-throated Solitaire in our hands. Parrots and parakeets lived there in large numbers, and the Cloud Swifts and the Red-necked Pigeons flew in bands. We sat for an hour one day on a big pile of sawdust and counted 58 species of birds.

One day we hiked up the hill for almost two hours. We came to a large flat that looked like a sea of blue. The wild forget-me-nots were in full bloom; against the dark green of the heavily forested hillsides, it was indeed a lovely sight. Dr. Kepler looked up to the cliffs that bordered the flat, and with an interested gleam in his eye asked, "Has anyone ever explored up there for the nest of the Black-capped Petrel?"

"What would a sea bird be doing on an inland mountain?" I asked.

"The Diablotín or the Black-capped Petrel is a most unusual bird," Dr. Kepler began. "It lives most of its life flying over the sea. It sleeps on the water, gets its food from the water, but it comes to land during the breeding season and then at night. The birds come first in courtship, flying over their nesting places, making strange and weird sounds that can be heard for long distances. They become involved in courtship flights and can be seen occasionally executing their complicated maneuvers by the light of the moon. When courtship is over, they gather in colonies to make deep burrows at the roots of pine trees on cliffs that have enough soil and pine duff in which to dig. Sometimes these nesting sites are located far from the sea, generally on the leeward side.

"Incubation takes an incredibly long time and the young are not fledged until they are completely feathered out."

"Have you ever seen one?" I asked. "Have you ever heard one sing?"

"I have seen them far out at sea," he said. "And I have heard them sing from a recording." He gave us an imitation of the wild, terrible call. It was a series of *a-a-a-a-a*s, or *aw-aw-aw-au*s, with croaks and hoarse squawks that would scare anyone caught out alone at night. No wonder the Dominican people call it the Diablotín! Diablotín, Diablo, the Devil!

"I have a report on the Black-capped Petrel that was written by David Wingate of Bermuda, who has done extensive work on them on his island. Would you like to have a copy of it? I can send it to you when I get home."

Dr. Kepler was as good as his word. It was not long before I had the report for study.

The article was a reprint taken from the *Auk*, (Vol. 81, No. 2, April 30, 1964) in which Dr. David Wingate told of the history of the *Pterodroma cahow* on Bermuda. A breeding colony had been found on the island in 1951, after many years of believing the bird had become extinct. Since he had particpated in the discovery and subsequent studies, he became interested in the closely related species, *Pterodroma hasitata*, whose breeding colonies had been lost to science since late in the 19th century. He thought the finding of the nesting colony on Bermuda boded well for the finding of *Pterodroma hasitata*. Perhaps some isolated colony might survive someplace in its former breeding range.

The story of his visit to Haiti, and his discovery of the colonies on Morne la Visite of the La Selle range was fascinating and very thought-provoking. The Sierra de Baoruco in the Dominican Republic is an extension of the La Selle Range and the Loma de Toro is one of the taller peaks in the range. Surely if the Black-capped Petrel were nesting in that range on the Haitian side, I reasoned, there were possibilities that it would be nesting on the Dominican side also.

We began to ask questions. No one had ever heard the raucous, loud voices, nor had anyone seen such a bird as we described. Finally one old man near the town of Puerto Escondido gave us a little hope. He came to visit us one evening as we were camped near a riverbed of a deep, dark canyon that came down from the Loma de Toro. When he saw that we were planning to stay there all night, he begged us to go someplace else.

"Sometimes we hear strange noises here," he said. "At night. This *arroyo* is not called the Devil's Canyon for nothing!"

We told him that we needed to get an early start the next day, and that nothing would hurt us. He became very agitated, and went away protesting our foolhardiness.

The next morning before we were up the old man returned. He was very surprised to find us still alive and well.

Several times I talked of making an expedition to the Loma de Toro in the winter time to find the nests of the Black-capped Petrel but we never did go. In August, 1979, when I received a letter from Dr. David Wingate himself asking if we would be interested in investigating "any areas that would be likely to have a colony of Black-capped Petrels," I was more than overjoyed. We would finally have an opportunity to search for the lost birds, and have an expert to help us as well!

The Director of the National Museum of Natural History where I was working was sympathetic to the idea, and the necessary measures were taken to set up an expedition. Included in our group were two British ornithologists, Roy Smith and Paul Andrews, graduates of Cambridge University in England; Miss Sue Riley, a devoted and enthusiastic birder; Tomás Vargas, ornithologist from the Wildlife Department; my husband from the National Botanical Garden; David Wingate from the Department of Agriculture of Bermuda and Helga Treadwell, president of the Audubon Society from the same island; and I.

It took three cars to carry us all, with our gear. We had an old Citroen, a middle-aged Volkswagen Beetle, and our Volkswagen bus. We were all heavily loaded and since our vehicles were not too dependable, we decided that we should stay together in case any of us should need help.

We were late in getting started on February 3, 1980, but we would have made it to the campground before dark if it had not been for an emergency stop. As our bus started up a steep grade, just over a mile below the Border Army Station, the steering apparatus failed. Luckily for us a tree that was strong enough to hold us up kept us from plunging over a bank.

We had already examined the car when the rest of our group showed up.

"What happened?" asked David and Helga.

"I think the bolt fell out of the steering mechanism, but I can't find it. I'll probably have to go back to the capital for parts!"

Then the Citroen drove up.

"Let me have a look at it," said Paul. As he walked toward the car, he continued, "If it is what I think it is, you are lucky that you were going uphill instead of down!"

He crawled under the car and after a few minutes came out saying, "I can fix it, but it will take a while. I've found the bolt."

We backed down to a wide place in the road, and there we made camp. After a few minutes, David Wingate said, "How far are we from the top?"

We gave him directions and they went on. They did not want to waste any time if it were not necessary.

We who stayed down at the lower level had a rather difficult night. The cars were parked on a slant, making it impossible to sleep on the level. We were cramped and cold, but finally dawn came and we could see. We made breakfast, and the "boys" went to work on the car. It was a great relief to know that Paul was more than an ornithologist. He was also a master mechanic!

Sue and I looked for birds after we had cleaned up the camp. We found a pair of trogons in courtship which were examining holes in trees in search of an adequate nesting place. We heard a Green-tailed Ground Warbler give its "bird-in-distress" call. We discovered that the Broad-billed Tody and the Narrow-billed Tody were sympatric in that area. About 10 o'clock we heard the "boys" call, "Everything is ready, let's go."

About the same time we heard the Volkswagen Beetle. What excitement it caused! Before they had stopped the car David and Helga yelled, "There must be a colony! We heard the Black-capped Petrels calling last night!"

With renewed vigor and determination we set out. But this time we had problems with the old Citroen. We towed it uphill with our bus in some of the tough places, until the rope broke. Then Paul drove in reverse on the steep grades. We finally arrived at the campground a bit before dark. We had to hurry to be ready for the night.

It was moonlight, which was a help. But it was cold, and we were all too tired to stay awake long, listening for night birds. However, about midnight we heard David call, "Listen, you can hear them now. They must be over in those cliffs!"

As deaf as I am without my hearing aids, I heard those weird, wild sounds. Our efforts had been rewarded!

For ten days we stayed at the camp. Two groups were organized to make overnight forays further east and south. Each day we studied the cliffs to see where the birds could be roosting, and during the day we'd plot places to visit on the cliffs. We did not have any luck finding the nests, nor other colonies of birds, but we heard the calls every night.

We discovered other things on the mountain. We found three horses gone wild, and we found their waterhole. We found arroyos where the Chat tanagers fed, and we watched them as they travelled through the understory of brush. We saw the La Selle's Thrush feed on earthworms in much the same manner as the American Robin. And Roy Smith discovered that the *Accipiter striatus* or Sharp-shinned Hawk was different from the one from North America.

We used the mist nets to determine the most common species; we took pictures; we looked for orchids. The days passed rapidly. By the end of the tenth day we had to admit we had not found the

Black-capped Petrel's nest, but we knew it came to the area. Had we come too early? Was the weather still too cold for nesting? On the way to the capital we made our plans for another year. We would go up later, and invite a mountain climber to be our guest.

Our second trip to Loma de Toro occurred in 1982 and a month later in the year. We had given such glowing reports of our stay on the mountain that more Dominicans wanted to participate in the venture.

José Alberto Ottenwalder, Tomás Vargas, and Adolfito Gottschalk represented three governmental institutions. Barry Phillips from Kew Gardens in London, a botanist; Richard Viet, a mountain climber from the University of Connecticut; Dr. David Wingate and Helga Treadwell from Bermuda; and Don and I completed the list of participants.

We had learned from our experience of 1980 and therefore selected our vehicles with more care but even though our bus was in good working order there was a limit to its power. Adolfito and I had to walk up several of the steep parts of the road because of loose rock.

We made our camp and that night we heard the Diablotines "sing" again. We thought the voices sounded stronger and we tried to plot on a map where the noises were the loudest. We traversed the trail from our camp to the top of the first ridge several times a night, leaving signs where we thought a colony might be. During the day the boys would climb the cliff. Later we would go to the top of the mountain in the jeep, then the boys would try to come down the face, looking for nests all along the way.

We had several adventures that week. We discovered that one of the wild horses had disappeared. We discovered that the Greater Antillean Elaena has a lovely dawn song, and that the Emerald Hummingbird takes the nectar from the pink flowered parasite of the pine trees. We saw a Crossbill break open a pine cone, but we were not close enough to get a good picture. We felt insecurity and worry one night when Adolfito and Barry were lost for a time in a dense forest. We were also anxious when one of our group felt the effect of the intense cold. Asthma and loss of body heat made it necessary to have emergency treatment, and on the following day he chose to go home.

During that week I felt frustration to the point of nausea. For two full years I had dreamed of obtaining a specimen of the Sharp-shinned Hawk *(Accipiter striatus)*. It had appeared to be very different from the North American form, and from the one I had known in Puerto Rico; I wanted to prove that we had an endemic subspecies on Hispaniola. We caught one in our mist net, a male of beautiful coloration, with the rufous red of the cheek patch and other parts in a contrast that I had never seen before. Oh, what a picture that would have made!

It was not difficult to release it from the net. We placed it in a small cotton sack to carry back to the photographer. In our excitement we did not tie the string well, nor did we close the car windows. When we reached for the sack, it was empty, The bird had escaped! Was I disgusted and disappointed!

My feelings were somewhat assuaged later, however, after I received an answer to my letter to Dr. James Bond telling him of my experience. He wrote, *"Accipiter striatus striatus* was originally described from Hispaniola. The ones you know from other places are the ones that have the rank of subspecies."

David Wingate and his party of hikers discovered a second Diablotín colony a few days before we left the area. And one night we had unexpected visitors. A pack train of several heavily loaded burros and a horse or two came up from the trail from Puerto Escondido. Evidently the people were Haitians and they must have been afraid of us. They whipped up their animals and passed us with great haste. We wondered what was in the sacks and what they had traded. We also wondered if they had been responsible for the disappearance of our wild horse.

Our trip down from the hill was uneventful but we enjoyed our camp-out at the lower level. We had no trouble keeping warm, even though we had a heavy shower. We were all able to see a Potoo fly over our camp, and alight on an old stub. We watched it assume the cryptic position through a special nocturnal telescope and we noted its owl-like face and its huge yellow eyes. The next day we observed a Golden Wing Warbler and a small group of Euphonias entertained us for a long time as they fed on the berries of the Mistletoe.

Two other trips were made that season to search for the colonies of the Diablotín. No signs of them were found on Pico Duarte, nor in the Sierra de Neiba. Nevertheless, we considered that our trips to the mountains were a great success.

Two weeks after our camping experience we read an article in the newspaper about a fire that had gone through Loma dc Toro. It burned for eight days before it was brought under control.

In May, 1983, we went back to our area. What a sad sight! Both sides of our campsite had been burned; dead pines stood everywhere; there was little underbrush for cover. Fortunately the little, broad, level copses were not affected nor had the cliff been touched. If the heat had not roasted the little birds, maybe some of them could have survived. However, we did not hear the birds calling. Maybe we were too late in the season.

Because of our reports, the area has been declared a National Park. Maybe someday it will be protected adequately. We can only hope that action did not come too late.

The Industrious Canopy Fisher

The Reddish Egret

Order:	Ciconiiformes
Family:	Ardeidae
Scientific name:	*Dichromanassa rufescens*
English name:	Reddish Egret
Spanish name:	Garza Rojiza

The salt water lagoons and marshes of the north coast are the least studied and known of the aquatic areas in the Dominican Republic, especially those in the northwest around Monte Cristi. The dryness of the area together with the xerophytic vegetation, heat and the isolation from all towns except Monte Cristi make it an unattractive place for camping. Additionally, the huge populations of mosquitoes and the ever-hungry, tiny "no-see-ums" make it an extremely hostile environment. Only the most motivated scientists or nature-lovers are willing to venture into the area. We had a wonderful time, however, when we first camped out in the place. In April 1975 we made an exploratory expedition along the border of Haiti and the Dominican Republic, going from Elias Pina to Bánica, then on to Pedro Santana. From there we drove 42 miles to Restauración before we saw another soul. We went on to Dajabón, and then to Monte Cristi. It took us several days to make the trip because the narrow road was far from an International Highway, as it is called. By the time we arrived in Monte Cristi, we were weary of riding over rough, steep roads. We were tired of seeing denuded hills and destroyed pine forests. The flat country, even if it was hot and dry, looked good to us.

We drove through the town until we came to El Morro Rock; it was near to the beach and close to the mangroves. We set up our camp late in the afternoon and took advantage of the evening bird activity. We noticed a few mosquitoes, but we daubed ourselves with repellent and enjoyed ourselves immensely.

The next morning we continued birding and we saw nearly everything in the book. Pelicans, migrant shore birds, herons, stilts, Common Gallinules, Ospreys, and Clapper Rails. Flocks of sandpipers held our interest for a long time. Of course we saw a few White-crowned Pigeons, Ground Doves, and a White-winged Dove or two. There were woodpeckers, cuckoos, todies, kingfishers. The Black-cowled Oriole was common as was the Black-whiskered Vireo. We saw many wintering warblers. What a bird paradise we had found! But even so, we did not see the Wood Stork. The last one recorded in the Dominican Republic was seen by me in this same area in 1966.

As we were getting ready to leave to make the last lap of our trip, a robust white heron with an interesting silhouette flew over our camp. I thought I was acquainted with all the white egrets, but this one was very confusing. The plumage appeared to be disorderly and as I looked at it through the binoculars, I saw its light bill tipped with black. Could it possibly be a rare Reddish Egret in the white phase? I had never before seen one, but I had seen this species in the dark form. I consulted the Field Guide.

According to the Field Guide, the Reddish Egret is distinguished from the common Little Blue Heron by its shaggy appearance, the light greenish feet, and the flesh-colored bill that is tipped with black. The head and neck are brick-red, disordered and bushy, while the Little Blue Heron is dark cinnamon-colored. The body of the Reddish Egret is brownish gray, while that of the Little Blue Heron is definitely darker bluish gray. The Egret is distinctly the larger bird. I also read that the Reddish Egrets often engage in canopy fishing. The Reddish Egret in its white phase has a bicolored bill and is very shaggy about the neck.

I had no time to study the white-phase egret further, as we needed to get started on our journey back to the capital.

We had many pleasant memories of that night spent in the mangrove swamps of Monte Cristi.

Then came the time when the National Museum of Natural History needed a specimen of the Clapper Rail for a diorama. Naturally we thought of the lagoons of Monte Cristi where we had seen the bird in numbers. In the first week of August 1977 we set out, remembering the activity and enjoyment of the previous trip. We were glad to have an excuse to go back.

We arrived late in the afternoon, just as the sun was going down. We located our old campground and opened the doors of the car to get out. It was as though we had opened the lid of Pandora's box. Hordes of biting insects descended upon us. We were thoroughly uncomfortable within minutes, dancing and battling to rid ourselves of fiendish things. We put on our long-sleeved shirts, buttoned up our collars, daubed ourselves with repellent, and tried to ignore them, but it was impossible. They almost carried us off bodily. They were in our hair, up our noses, crawling at our eyelids, buzzing in our ears, seeking moisture from our lips. When we opened our mouths to eat, we ate insect protein along with our food. Our bodies felt as though they were on fire, because the insects bit through our clothing. We tried to escape them by going to bed. We put up the mosquito nets and shut all the windows of the car. We rolled ourselves in sheets with only our nostrils out enough so we could breathe. The little devils came through the nets and hummed and buzzed around us all night. It was so humid and so hot that we were most uncomfortable and we certainly did not sleep much. We decided to leave the mangrove as soon as we could obtain the specimen for the museum.

But as it always does, the dawn came. And with it came a cool breeze that carried away many of the pests. We were able to enjoy the wide variety of bird life. We were happy to see the Great Blue Heron in its white phase, and after hunting for a while in the dense mangroves we obtained a specimen of the Clapper Rail, in spite of another uncomfortable session with the no-see-ums.

After we had returned to camp, in the very late morning, a white heron flew over the camp. It alighted in the shallow water and stood very still for a few minutes. I thought I might be seeing the Reddish Egret in its white phase but when it began to fish, I was certain. I had read of the canopy fishing, but I had never actually seen that kind of activity. What luck, because I had a ring-side seat!

The Reddish Egret flew over an area of shallow water, obviously looking for prey. When it came to a school of fish, it alighted some distance away, then with long strides it slowly walked toward the area where it must have seen the fish. The head and neck were lifted up as if the bird was on the alert. After stalking for a short distance, the bird stopped, gave a half-turn, raised up its wings, ran a few steps, jumped into the air, landed, gave another half-turn, then suddenly struck out at its victim.

This bird fished for such a long time I was beginning to get tired. Some other white herons flew in, and the attention of the fishing egret was diverted. It certainly put up a great defense of its territory, for the intruders were dispatched without much ceremony.

In its white phase, the Reddish Egret is spectacular. Completely white, with shaggy feathers and a large bushy head, it is set apart from any of the other white herons. It is a bird of the coastal areas, of salt-water flats and mangroves. As I stood watching its show, several questions came to mind. Why is the white-phased Reddish Egret seen more frequently in the Dominican Republic than the colored one? Do the colored-phased birds and the birds in the white phase interbreed? Are the white-phased birds albinos? Why is the Reddish Egret so rare in all parts of its range?

I did not have time to contemplate answers. My husband insisted that we leave before the breeze went down. Our experience with the insects of the previous night was not easily forgotten! We broke camp and moved to the mountains.

That night we camped by a clear, rushing stream. After taking a cleansing, refreshing bath, and eating our evening meal in peace, our good humor was restored and we were able to laugh at our suffering from the biting insects.

We never again returned to the mangroves of Monte Cristi in the month of August!

An Endangered Species

The West Indian Whistling Duck

Order:	Anseriformes
Family:	Anatidae
Scientific name:	*Dendrocygna arborea*
English name:	West Indian Whistling Duck
Spanish name:	La Yaguaza

We have four species of ducks on the island of Hispaniola. The largest and the one with the smallest population is the West Indian Whistling Duck, or *Dendrocygna arborea*. Time was when this beautiful duck was abundant. It lived in all the swamps and lagoons of the country; it inhabited the rice fields and the mangrove swamps. But that time is gone forever. Because of over-hunting, the destruction of its habitat, egg-robbing, and the use of insecticides in the rice fields, its numbers have declined alarmingly. Hunters complain because there are none left to hunt, not realizing that they are chiefly responsible for the bird's demise. The Whistling Duck appears to be a combination of duck, goose, and swan. Its appearance is that of a goose, its breeding behavior is like that of a swan, but it has physical characteristics and habits that relate it to ducks. It can easily walk on dry land and the male helps the female with the work of incubation.

The West Indian Whistling Duck makes its nest on the ground but sometimes the nest is made in a tree house where there are bromeliads. Ten to fourteen eggs are laid, and the incubation period is up to 40 days.

When the nest is made in a tree, the duck has a unique way of getting the babies down to the ground. One of the parents will fly down to the ground while the other one stays by the nest. When they are ready, the one in the nest pushes a nestling out to have it fall on the back of the duck on the ground, thus breaking its fall. Often the adult will take the little one on its back for a ride.

Whistling Ducks are mostly nocturnal, becoming active at dusk and moving around until daybreak. It is a thrilling sight to see a band of ducks pass overhead and hear their clear, strong whistle. During the day they rest in bands in trees near water.

The West Indian Whistling Ducks have been accused of damaging the rice crops by flying in and weighing down the rice plants with their weight. I personally feel that has been an excuse to overhunt, because the bird is very good eating and is large. An ordinary duck weighs up to three or four pounds.

The West Indian Whistling Duck is a beautiful bird that can be recognized by its silhouette, with long legs, long neck and heavy body. Its general color is a dull brown on its upper parts with paler margins on most of the feathers that give the bird a squamated appearance. The throat is white and the foreneck is finely streaked with dusky. The upper breast is dull brown. The abdomen is buffy; the lower breast, the sides, and the tail are buffy white spotted with black. The beak is black and the feet and legs are greenish.

For many years, its relative the *Dendrocygna bicolor* or the Fulvous Tree Duck from South America was considered a migrant in the Dominican Republic. We found its nest in the lagoon in Monte Cristi so now it is considered a resident. It is a much smaller bird than the preceding species, weighing from two to three pounds. It is much brighter in color, being brick-red with black on the wings and on the back. There is white on the tail, flanks and sides.

The Fulvous Tree Duck is called the *Yaguasín* locally and it lives in the same habitat as the West Indian Whistling Duck. These birds are easily domesticated and are often seen in private patios in the northwest. Many people rob the eggs to place them under a hen so they will hatch out in captivity. Their call is a clear whistle similar to that of the West Indian Whistling Duck but not as strong or loud. Their conversational chatter is most agreeable and can be heard for some distance.

A Seldom-seen Duck

The White-cheeked Pintail

Order: Anseriformes
Family: Anatidae
Scientific name: *Anas bahamensis*
English name: White-cheeked Pintail
                    (Bahamian Pintail)
Spanish name: Pato de la Orilla

The White-cheeked Pintail is a beautiful duck. The brown and light brown squamated appearance of the body, the darker brown wings, the iridescent green and buffy patch, white cheeks and bright yellow bill distinguish it from the other native ducks. The only other duck that is similar is the migratory green-winged teal but the pointed, buffy tail is a distinguishing characteristic. The sexes are similar.

These attractive little ducks were at one time plentiful in the Dominican Republic and were widely distributed in lagoons near the coast and in marshes of fresh water. Sometimes they were found in ponds in the savannas, or rushes or tules. But over-hunting and egg- hunting have taken their toll. At the present time, the bird is seldom seen.

Once, in February, we made a bird and orchid study excursion to the southwestern coast of the Dominican Republic. During that trip we made our camp one night in the short, stunted, dry forest not far from the small fishing village of Oviedo. Early in the morning we visited the Lagoon of Oviedo.

What surprises awaited us that day! We walked for about 15 minutes through a bushy, fleshy, succulent-like plant that has a most peculiar smell. We found a beautiful blue-tailed lizard, hermit crabs, a skink or two, and—wonder of all wonders—old dead trees that were literally covered with an orchid named *Broughtonia domingensis*. After we got over our surprise, we continued on to the lagoon where we were fortunate to see some Roseate Spoonbills feeding, the Louisiana Heron, the Snowy Egret with its golden slippers, and a good-sized group of White-cheeked Pintails—more than 30, at least.

We had a most extraordinary show. Some of the birds were in breeding condition. Their yellow bills had turned color and some were bright orange to almost a brilliant red. There was a good deal of activity. Some birds on the bank were taking advantage of the morning sun, while others were oiling their feathers. A few were at the edge of the water among the mangrove roots. But the ones in the water were in action! One bird was swimming in circles around another. The feathers were raised and the head somewhat lowered. The bill was dipped into the water and then it was passed through the feathers on the bird's breast. The neck was stretched, the beak was dipped into the water again, and when the head was raised, the water ran out of the sides of the beak. There were whistles, to which the second bird responded. Finally the first began to swim after the second (the male and female are very similar in appearance), making funny noises. Then there were bows, head twisting and wing flapping, and the female accepted the male. The nests are hidden in the vegetation or between the roots of the mangrove trees. As many as 12 buffy-colored eggs are laid, with the female doing all the work. According to James Bond, the female quacks and the drake has a low squeaky call. The only vocalization I heard was the "conversation" during the courtship ritual.

The Bahamian Pintail is found in the Bahamas, Cuba and Hispaniola, from Puerto Rico to the Virgin Islands and the northern Lesser Antilles, also on islands in South America including Trinidad and Tobago, and in continental South America. It is casual in Florida.

A Helpful, Endangered Friend

The Ridgway's Hawk

Order:	Falconiformes
Family:	Accipitridae
Scientific name:	*Buteo ridgwayi*
English name:	Ridgway's Hawk
Spanish name:	Gavilán

Los Haitises is a special name for a special environment on the north coast of the Dominican Republic. The name is supposed to be derived from an Indian word, "haiti," meaning rocky place. The area is characterized by deep, narrow valleys between steep hills that reach a maximum height of about 1,000 feet. The formation is of karst limestone which is frequently ledged. There are many caves, few rivers, occasional springs, and much rainfall. In between the precipitous hills where there is a good depth of soil, there is an exuberant plant growth—a good example of a jungle. There grow the tall broadleaf forests, many species of ferns and mosses, vines and epiphytes.

Immediately above the luxuriant growth of the valley, the vegetation is radically different. The heavy rainfall drains away rapidly, leaving little leaf mould or soil on the rocks. Where the rock is solid, cacti, spiny bushes and other examples of xerophytic plants grow. However, wherever a crack or a seepage develops, enterprising trees insert their roots and thus find sustenance for a larger growth. Along the exterior of the cliffs the tall, broad strangler fig trees take advantage of the accumulation of leaf mould. Their root systems are exposed as they grow down to seek the moisture of the lower level. (These roots are very important to an explorer as they can be used as ladders to move from one level to another.) Because of the peculiar ecology, and the wide variety of flora, the fauna and avifauna are most interesting. And because of the difficult terrain, the remoteness and so many unknowns, the area has remained relatively unexplored until recently.

During Trujillo's time the hills of Los Haitises were used as a sanctuary by many a person who found himself in disfavor with the regime. A fugitive had little or no trouble living off the land, according to one old man whom we found on a trail about two hours walk from Pilancón. He told us that the caves offered good shelter from the elements. He killed birds with rocks or a slingshot. He trapped for wild pigs and hunted the endemic spiny rat that looks like a big guinea pig. He gathered the abundant wild fruit and root vegetables to round out his very adequate diet. He held us fascinated as he told his story, making us relive with him some of the experiences he had had during the seven years that he had hidden from Trujillo in the interior of the hills.

In 1973 we began our serious studies in Los Haitises. We were forbidden to go into the Cordillera Central because a guerrilla group had arrived from Cuba and set up a camp in the area of our previous investigations.

We entered the mountains from the north, south, east and west. We made many new friends, discovered plants new to science, and found a rare species of gecko lizard, the male of which has never been found. We saw the marks on the bark of a tree that were made by the near-extinct, endemic rodent, the *Plagiodontia aedi*. I was presented with a beautiful pair of tusks taken from a wild boar and was offered a dish of the stew. After sampling the tough, stringy, strong-tasting meat, and judging from the size of the tusks, I came to the conclusion that the animal had been a mighty old boar.

We were taken completely by surprise by the bird life. We found species that we had known to exist only in the high mountains of the Cordillera Central, the Sierra de Baoruco, and the Sierra de Neiba. Birds such as the Solitaire, the Stripe-headed Tanager, and the Emerald Hummingbird were present. The Narrow-billed Tody was living side-by-side with the Broad-billed Tody. The parrots and parakeets were everywhere, as well as the White-necked Crow. We found the migrant Worm-eating Warbler was abundant; other species of brightly colored winter residents added excitement and variety to our trips. We saw the Rose-breasted Grosbreak in the tall trees and the Blue Grosbeak and the bright red male Summer Tanager in the more humid areas. We noted that every one of our birds of prey, with the exception of the Burrowing Owl, lives in Los Haitises. We had the incredible luck of finding the nest of the endemic and endangered Ridgway's Hawk *(Buteo ridgwayi)*.

In February, 1968, we were traveling between Sabana Grande de Boya and Arenosa, going to the west side of the River Yuna. It had not rained for some time, and the river was too low for us to use the ferry but still too high to ford. So we had to pass the night on the west side of the river by the side of the road that winds in and out among the hills and the valleys of the Haitises country. As luck would have it, we made our camp by a trail that led up a very steep hill. Naturally we wanted to see what was on the other side! Early the next morning we climbed the trail using the vegetation to pull ourselves along when our precarious footholds would not allow us to go forward with assurance. Needless to say, it was quite a climb. When we reached the top and looked down on the valley below, we were sickened by the destruction that had recently taken place. A tractor had been through; men were chopping the ancient trees that had been felled, in preparation for making charcoal. Some of the old stumps were still smoldering from the fires that had been set days before.

In spite of the destruction many species of birds were flying, singing and calling. We saw Plain Pigeons, Mourning Doves, and Palm Chats; all three species of hummingbirds were there. We saw the two species of todies, both vireos and many migrant warblers.

In no time at all my husband found a place to look for orchids. I continued on alone on the trail that led to a rather wide *arroyo*. And there my day was made! I came across a pair of Ridgway's Hawks in courtship and they were building a nest.

My attention was first attracted to a large bird flying low up the *arroyo*, coming directly toward me. It had a long (about 15 inches), slim twig grasped in its talons. As it came closer, it veered a bit, passed me and swooped up to a branch of a huge strangler fig tree. Just before it landed, it squealed and then I saw the other bird move. It was obviously the mate. It was waiting beside a partially constructed nest that was situated in a clump of bromeliads, about 40 feet above the ground. When the first bird deposited its twig, the mate began to look for a place to put it, turning around and around as if shaping the nest. I found a good log in the shade and after searching for centipedes and finding none, I sat down to watch.

I had a good chance to see the differences between the two sexes. One was larger than the other and of drab coloration; I took this to be the female. The general plumage was brownish gray, with brown on the wings. The underparts were light orange and were slightly barred. The smaller bird was colorful, with brick-colored thighs and with patches of the same color on the wings; the chin was white.

One bird was in the nest and the other one nearby when suddenly the female flew down to a dead branch on a tree not far from the nest tree. She squealed several times and then the male came and struck her with such force that she nearly lost her grip on the perch. After much wing flapping by the female to get her balance, the male mounted her and they copulated. The male then flew off while the female stayed for nearly 20 minutes arranging her feathers and sunning herelf. Neither bird went back to the nest while I was observing.

Jim and Beth Netherly Wiley, field biologists from Puerto Rico, conducted a parrot study in the Haitises from January to June 1976. At the same time they were able to make the first real scientific study of the life history of the diminishing Ridgway's Hawk. As a result of their work they made a brilliant report which was published in the *Condor* in November, 1981.

In April, 1978, my husband and I were again back in Los Haitises. We found a nest of the Ridgway's Hawk with two white, fluffy nestlings. The nest was high in a tall tree, on top of a pile of twigs that proved to be the home of a colony of Palm Chats. Both species were feeding young and living together in peace.

We wanted to look down into the hawk's nest to observe what the parent birds brought to their young. To do this, we had to climb a terrace above the nest. Amidst a great deal of suppressed laughter, we helped each other up the exposed roots of a tree that was conveniently situated on a cliff across the *arroyo* from the nest.

Our activity seemed to agitate the birds. There were many alarm notes and screams given, and even after we waited for some time they did not calm down. We decided to make a blind.

We went back to our camp, sewed some sacks together and returned to the nesting site. I helped my husband hide himself and the camera under the sacks and then I went away. Evidently the birds did not know how to count because my departure left them satisfied that no one was around, and they went about their work. After several hours of waiting and observing, my husband was able to take some very satisfactory pictures and learned that the parent birds brought several rats and a snake to their chicks.

Much of the wild area of the Haitises has been destroyed. The common cultivated crop is the yautia, a type of "Elephant Ear" that is widely used in the tropics as a starch. When you have root vegetables, naturally the rats are present. Because of the rats there are birds of prey, hawks and owls. And if the raptors were left alone, there would be effective control of the rats. But nay, not so in the Haitises. The superstitious farmers are afraid of the raptors and whenever possible they will kill them on sight.

It is believed that the hawks eat chickens and are dangerous. Owls are thought to have supernatural powers and are enemies of the people. Owls try to mate with the hens; if they are not successful, the aggressor eats out the eyes and leaves the hen to die. The raptors are accused of spreading fatal diseases among the flocks of domesticated fowl. Superstitions, habitat loss, agricultural fires and uncontrolled hunting are responsible for our diminishing bird life.

Conservationists on our island are worried about the future of our birds of prey. Unless we have a program of environmental education soon, in the areas where the damage is being done I do not have much hope for the survival of the endemic and endangered Ridgway's Hawk.

A Prediction Fulfilled

The Spotted Rail

Order:	Gruiformes
Family:	Rallidae
Scientific name:	*Pardirallus maculatus*
English name:	Spotted Rail
Spanish name:	Gallito Manchado

Soon after the ornithologists Dr. Cameron Kepler and his wife, Dr. Kay Kepler from Puerto Rico came to visit us in March of 1972, I began my search for a new bird on the island of Hispaniola. The Keplers had recently announced a new-to-science warbler, *Dendroica angelae* found in the Elfin Forest of the Luquillo National Forest in Puerto Rico. After hearing the story of how they made their discovery, I thought that if they had found a new species on a densely populated, well-studied small island like Puerto Rico, surely I should be able to find something new on Hispaniola. Hispaniola is eight times as large as Puerto Rico and is not as densely populated. There had been no intensive ornithological studies made since the time of James Bond and Alexander Wetmore (1927-1931).

During this time the Dominican Republic was undergoing a severe population explosion and there was much cutting and burning of forests. In spite of this, there was still some virgin territory left in remote areas where a new, hard-to-see bird could be hiding out. I was so sure I would find something new that I even mapped out a plan for searching.

I began by writing to Dr. James Bond. author of the Field Guide to the Birds of the West Indies. His reply to my letter was immediate, and I shall never forget my excitement as I read it over and over again. I read it so many times that it became dog eared and grimy. I carried it in the glove compartment of the van for several years.

Dr. Bond (as I remember it) said in his letter,"l did most of my work on Hispaniola in Haiti. I do not speak Spanish, but I am fluent in French. Another factor in determining where I studied was your ill-famed dictator, Trujillo. I was allowed to stay in the country only four days, so I went to the Samana Peninsula where many of the ornithologists before me had worked. When my time was up, I rode my horse along the trails back to Haiti. Between the four days and the ride back, I got a fair idea of the bird life of the Dominican Republic."

"Offhand I would say that the swamps, the low wetlands, and the forests at the sides of the ricefields were less studied than any of the other habitats. I saw very few rails; the Clapper was quite common, but the little Yellow Crake was difficult to locate. For the size of Hispaniola, there should be other rails. The Spotted is known in the Dominican Republic only from bones found in caves, but has not been reported in modern times. The Little Black Rail has never been reported from Hispaniola but should be expected since it is found in Cuba, and at one time was common on Jamaica. New species can be found anywhere! Look what the Keplers found in Puerto Rico. Good luck! Sincerely, James Bond.

It took me several years to do it, but we finally discovered the Spotted Rail in the Dominican Republic, the first report ever from Hispaniola.

It came about in a very unexpected way. Early one morning in 1978 I received an urgent telephone call from a colleague, who was working for the Department of Agriculture. He said he had a live bird in his backyard that two boys had brought in to me for identification. They had come in from the country the day before but they couldn't find our house. They gave the bird to him to care for. Would I please come and get it?

Naturally my husband and I went at once, armed with the field guide to the Birds in the West Indies. We tried to guess what kind of a bird it was as we drove across town. We found my colleague waiting at the gate.

"Where is it? Tell me all you know about it, please.

"It is happy and contented in my back yard, looking for its breakfast. I clipped its wing so it can't fly away."

"What does it look like?" I asked.

"It looks like a little spotted chicken with a long bill. Come with me."

"I am willing to bet it is the Spotted Rail!" I told my husband.

As we rounded the corner of the house, we saw many caged birds on a cement floor under a makeshift roof. The racket was deafening. The birds included Japanese quail, Bob Whites, several kinds of pigeons, ground doves and even some game cocks. They had been fed and every bird was declaring territory. After I had adjusted myself a bit, I asked, "But where is the new bird?"

"Under the cages, over there!"

And sure enough there it was, the Spotted Rail, just as Dr. James Bond had predicted. You could not mistake it. *Pardirallus maculatus*, page 69. It was a striking, beautifully marked bird. The plumage was black, spotted with white, the abdomen striped, the back and wings washed with brown, the bill green, with a bright red spot at the base of the lower mandible, and the feet red.

I showed the picture in Bond's book to my colleague, Don Miguel. All three of us agreed that it was the Spotted Rail. When I told him we had never seen it alive before, he said, "Then it must be new for our country." So with the verification of both Don Miguel and mv husband, I dared to report it in my weekly Nature Column in the Saturday Supplement of *El Caribe*, one of the two large daily papers in Santo Domingo. I sent the article to James Bond.

After that announcement I made a special effort to find the young fellow who had originally discovered the bird. I found him working in a bank in San Francisco de Marcoris. He told me that he and two friends had been enjoying a day in the country near a village called Arenoso. They passed a freshly ploughed field where a farmer was making a new rice paddy. Several birds of the same species were cowering in a patch of grass in the center of the field still unplowed. The birds tried to hide instead of flying, and the boys caught several with their bare hands.

We were later able to obtain other specimens for the National Museum of Natural History. We added to the scientific collection and used one example in a diorama. Dr. George Reynard was able to record its voice and John Clements and his wife flew to the Dominican Republic to see the one still in captivity.

Don Miguel finally gave our live specimen to the Zoological Park where it lived for several months before it suffered an accident that proved fatal.

A Bird That Lives in the Habitat of a Rat

The Black Rail

Order:	Gruiformes
Family:	Rallidae
Scientific name:	*Laterallus jamaicensis*
English name:	Black Rail
Spanish name:	El Bien Escondido,
	El Gallito Negro

One day a colleage with whom I had been working in the environmental education program said to me, "Mrs. Dod, I have read your big bird book from cover to cover and I have been using your field guide to our birds ever since it was published. There is a small bird that I used to know in the *campo* when I was a child that you have not mentioned. I have not seen it for many years. I wonder if it's extinct. Do you know what bird I am talking about?" "What did the bird look like, Freddy? Maybe I can recognize it if you could give me a description." "Well," said Freddy, "It is a little bird. It is dark and speckled black and white. It runs among the tall grasses, in the undergrowth, where there is dampness. It lives like a rat, running through the vines."

"What is its form? Tell me about the feet and the beak."

"Well," said Freddy again, "It is a 'ciguita,' a little bird, like I said. It is very small with a fairly long bill. The feet are like those of a little bird, but it has long toes."

"Because of its habitat, I would guess that it belongs to the family of rails *(Rallidae)* but I would have to see it," I said. "The rails are water birds that are adapted to live in the savannas where there are pools and puddles of water. Their bills are moderately long, and their feet and legs are too, because many times they walk on water plants, like water lilies. They also walk in between the grasses where there are muddy places, searching for food. They even nest among the reeds and cattails. Their life histories are not well-known, as they live a secret life—all covered up!"

"That sounds like my little bird. When I was a child I used to ride horseback through the grasses and plants on the savannas. I'd see the birds fly up to the level of the plants, then 'fall out' of the air. We'd never be able to find them again. They would run through the plants like rats."

Again I insisted that I would have to see the little bird, but I was sure it was a member of the rail family. I had heard other people mention a little black rail and I was sure Freddy had something interesting and probably new. When I told Freddy that, he laughed long and loud. "You are always looking for something new and different for the island," he said.

"Yes, I am," I answered candidly. "With an island like ours, with so many interesting environments and combinations of habitats, there are many possibilities. It is very worthwhile to investigate everything. You must find me a specimen."

Almost a year later, on the morning of December 30, 1984, I received a telephone call from Freddy. He told me he had a specimen for me!

I could hardly contain my excitement.

"Bring it to me, Freddy," I yelled. "Bring it right away!" In less than an hour Freddy appeared, carefully carrying a small box perforated with holes and tied up with a strong string. In our excitement we began to open the box until I restrained him. "Don't open the box out here! Take it into the bathroom where there are no open windows!"

When we had all the windows of the house closed and a light on, we opened the box little by little. There inside we saw a small black bird sitting in a corner. As soon as the light penetrated inside, the little creature stood up and began to walk around. Freddy caught it in his hand. When I saw the beak and the feet, I was sure of the identification. It was a very much alive little Black Rail, *Laterallus jamaicensis*. It had never been reported before from the island of Hispaniola.

We put the bird in a wire cage so it could have some fresh air. We got a cupful of bird food from a neighbor and put a dish of water into the cage. The bird began to eat at once. We also got some material out of our compost pile and put in some grass. The bird began to make noises to let us know it was content.

We took pictures and after a long discussion decided we had better go visit the area where the bird had been captured. We closed up the house and started out to the savanna between Monte Plata and Bayaguana. When we got to the little village of Monte Plata, we found the young man, Carlos Jiménez Beato, who had brought the bird to Freddy. He showed us the way to the pasture near the River Yaví.

I recognized the area. We had passed the night there several different times recording the songs of nocturnal birds as well as other night noises. How could we have passed up the little Black Rail?

We walked all around the pasture. There were many acres that had been plowed and planted to the African Oil palms. In between the rows, tropical kudzu had been planted as ground cover. We finally came to a place that had not been disturbed. There were tall plants of various kinds of grasses, and close to the ground many kinds of vines like morivivir, condeamor, and convulvulus were growing. There we stopped.

"Over there in the pasture where those horses are is the place we found the bird," Carlos said. "I saw four that day. My companion saw another three. I think there are many in this place because the birds are concentrated in the undisturbed area, as a result of the damage that the plow has done to their environment."

Suddenly Freddy gave us a sign to be still.

"I heard a peep," he said. "There is one close by."

Then the fellows gave us a good demonstration of how to capture a little rail, but they were not successful.

"It isn't easy," they said. "The birds do not like to fly."

Before we started home we collected some tall grasses and characteristic vines and plants to put in with our caged bird. We wanted to simulate a natural environment.

The next day we took more pictures and then Freddy took his treasure to the Zoological Park, where it lived happily for almost a week. One morning it was found dead on the floor of the cage.

The specimen was given to the National Museum of Natural History, where it is now in the Scientific Collection with the number 1679.

The following is the relevant scientific report, reprinted from American Birds:

The Black Rail *(Laterallus Jamaicensis)* in Hispaniola

On December 30, 1984, Freddy Soriano, an educator in the Zoological Park of Santa Domingo, brought me a tiny, live rail for identification. It had been caught by a *campesino* in a field which was being plowed between Monte Plata and Bayaguana. I readily recognized the bird as being a Black Rail *(Laterallus jamaicensis)*, the first record from Hispaniola, although known from the other three major islands of the Greater Antilles. The specimen is now #1679 in the collection of the Museo Nacional de Historia Natural in Santo Domingo. Later that day I was taken to the place by the young man who had captured the rail and both he and Freddy assured me the species was numerous in the area near the Río Yaví. Small ponds and puddles were scattered among tall grass *(Andropogon)*, beneath which was a tangled mass of vines.

Black Rails of eastern North America are classified as *L.j. jamaicensis*, indistinguishable from those of the Greater Antilles (A.O.U. *Check-list*, ed. 5, 1957, p. 158), the latter considered indigenous and non-migratory. However, James Bond informs me that two individuals were picked up in an exhausted condition on the beach at Marianao in suburban Havana and taken to the Zoological Gardens of that city where they thrived for many months on a diet gleaned from large chunks of black swamp mulch changed every two days. Therefore, at least some of these rails are apparently winter residents in the West Indies. There is as yet no evidence that the species breeds on the islands. The lack of recent records from Jamaica and Puerto Rico is doubtless due to mongoose predation, for this carnivore is far more numerous and widespread there than in Cuba and Hispaniola.

I wish to thank James Bond and George B. Reynard for their help with and contribution to this report.

Adios, Beautiful

The White-crowned Pigeon

Order:	Columbiformes
Family:	Columbidae
Scientific name:	*Columba leueucephala*
English name:	White-crowned Pigeon
Spanish name:	Paloma Coronita, Paloma Coquito Blanco

The White-crowned Pigeon was once very common throughout the Greater Antilles, appearing in nesting flocks of tens of thousands. Older *campesinos* still speak of the darkening skies when the big flocks flew over their area. But in recent years the population has declined in nearly every part of its range. The absence of the birds gives the naturalists great cause for worry because the once very abundant Passenger Pigeon of North America followed the same pattern. Uncontrolled hunting and the constant destruction of its habitat were and are responsible for the diminishing numbers.

During our numerous trips into the interior of the island, we have seen small numbers of this beautiful, blue-gray pigeon with its silvery crown in the woodlands of the North, South, East and West. But during the springtime, after the first heavy rains which mark the end of the dry season, large numbers of these birds appear as if by magic in the coastal areas. They form flocks soon after their arrival, choose a nesting site, and start building. The colony is called a *banco* and will sometimes number up into the hundreds of nesting pairs. The loud, deep calls of "Cro-cru-cru-cru-co-coo" can be heard over a long distance. The rustic nest is constructed of dry twigs that are thrown together with utter abandon, with sometimes as many as fifty nests in one tree. One wonders how such a haphazard, fragile structure can possibly support the weight of the parent bird and the eggs or nestlings. Two shiny white eggs are laid; incubation takes only 12 days and the birds fledge when one month old.

The nervous temperament of the White-crowned Pigeon is not favorable for great nesting success. If the *bancos* are disturbed, the birds abandon the site, leaving the nests in whatever stage of development. Many people used to attack the colonies when there were squabs, which they gathered and used as pig feed. Although there are laws against such practices, it is difficult to patrol remote areas against illegal hunting and many times the wardens seem to be less than honest. As a consequence, there is poor nesting success and therefore a low rate of reproduction.

However, at this moment, we have reason to be encouraged about the future of the White-crowned Pigeon in the Dominican Republic. A new administration has made the public more conservation- conscious. Some of our old laws are being updated and environmental education is being emphasized. There is better cooperation among the various governmental institutions in regard to the wise use of our natural resources. But best of all, new areas have been set aside for national parks where the endangered flora, fauna, and avifauna will be protected and allowed to procreate in peace.

My first encounter with large numbers of White-crowned Pigeons came when we visited the Bay of San Lorenzo in August, 1976. The program committee of the Dominican Orchid Society wanted us to check the area as a possible site for group orchid study. We were only too glad to have an excuse to go there.

We drove our van to Sabana de la Mar, where we talked to a Forestry Service man who helped us find a guide who had a boat with an outboard motor. The fellow told us of a place where we could camp in a cave and make forays out into the bay, as well as study the shoreline and places farther back into the forest.

Our guide told us that two men were living in the cave, and that they were there to protect the interests of a person who had tried to make a tourist attraction out of the area. The person had run out of money, and had to abandon the project half finished. The guide assured us that "Juan" and "José," the caretakers, would be very happy to have visitors.

Although there were still a few unknowns, we decided we'd take a chance. We bought gasoline and oil for the motorboat and proceeded in our car to a place called Bambu on the west side of a little village called Caño Hondo. There we left our Volkswagen, carried all our gear to the motorboat, and started out. We went through some of the most beautiful mangroves I have ever seen. At every twist or turn in the waterway, a little Green-backed Heron or a Great Egret would fly out, disturbed by us intruders. American Redstarts, brilliant in any season of the year, were everywhere. Other brightly colored birds flew in and out of the trees: green and red Todies, bright yellow Warblers, black and red Greater Antillean Bull-finches, and now and then a Black-crowned Palm Tanager with its mate would greet us with the familiar "Guiro" call. We saw Black- crowned Night Herons and a few "pintos": Pinto is the name given to the young Little Blue Herons that are changing from white to adult plumage.

It didn't take us long to reach the open bay. We continued west, staying close to the edges of the rugged limestone banks and cliffs that were covered with vegetation. There was much maidenhair fern, an occasional orchid called *Bletia patula,* many mangrove trees, strangler fig, and other broadleaf species unknown to me. In about 15 minutes we were at a small dock at the "Cueva de Arena," which means Sand Cave. The caretakers were not home, but we unloaded our gear anyway, confident that we would be welcome. Then we went out in the motorboat to investigate our surroundings.

Our guide was a talented storyteller. We sat on the edge of our seats as he told us of the early history of the bay. He showed us a cave where a young couple had made their home for many years, living off the fruits of the forest and the fresh fish from the waters of the Bay. The young wife had even given birth to their first child in the cave. We saw where some Englishmen had constructed a railroad over 100 years ago, to carry their agricultural products to a deck where some old pilings now provided resting-places for brown pelicans. We passed a forest-covered cayo (rock) that was home to hundreds of water birds. When we went by in the motorboat they rose up in clouds: Magnificent Frigatebirds, herons, pelicans, gray Kingbirds, one lone, two-toned Brown Booby, and many White- crowned Pigeons. Nearby, on another cayo we saw Turkey Vultures and White-necked Crows.

Our guide was greatly impressed because we could recognize all the birds. When I told him of our studies and work in conservation he said,"I know we need a complete educational plan for our whole nation. It is with sadness that I tell you this true story.

"During the month of May some hunters came here to look for the White-crowned Pigeons. The pigeons had not arrived yet as the rains were late, and the absence of the birds caused one of the men to become very angry. He had made a long trip to hunt pigeons and there was none to hunt. He took out his frustrations and desire for vengeance by shooting and killing about 150 frigatebirds. Most of them were in courtship or already nesting. We knew because many males had the red gular sack inflated. The dead birds were floating everywhere in the water."

"Why didn't you submit them to justice?" I asked angrily.

"What good does it do? I am sure there must be something wrong with our Justice Department! When we arrest someone for breaking the hunting laws, the lawbreakers are given a very small fine of only $5.00. Then the hunters laugh at us and say that hunting is more fun and lots cheaper than going to a movie!"

The salty breezes and the hour were giving us a good appetite. When the guide took us back to the Sand Cave we found that the caretakers had arrived. What a delicious feast they had prepared for us! Fresh fish, fried in coconut oil squeezed recently from the nut. After a little rest, the "owners" of the cave helped us with our gear, giving us instructions as to where to make our camp and how to fix our beds in the cave.

We stayed in this miniature paradise for three nights and three days. At night the cave was completely free of obnoxious insects, for the bats kept it swept clean. We could feel their wings fan our faces as we lay on our sleeping bags in the sand. The little crabs nibbled our fingers and toes when we'd stick them out from under the sheet. One night we had what we thought was an electrical storm. We got up to see what made the lights at the mouth of the cave. They were caused by the rain falling on the surface of the water, which was populated by millions of tiny dynaflagellae. These organisms, on being disturbed by rain or a fish, react by giving off a flood of light that illuminates the water like a fairy-land.

During the day we made forays into the woods, or out into the bay in the cayuco. We saw a cat gone wild, a flock of guinea fowl, and many of the common birds. We also found many species of orchids. On one little *cayo* hardly a yard above the level of the water, my husband saw some plants that interested him. He had our paddler put the dugout up to the edge, and then clambered up the coral rock. On top, among some shrubs, he found a mat of orchid plants, *Encyclia olivacea*, some in bloom. There was a thick mat of them and in trying to pull up a few he discovered that they had propagated themselves, their reclining flower stems rooting at the nodes to produce other plants. Never before had he seen this happen to this species that generally grows epiphytically.

Along the water's edge we saw little fish and many kinds of tiny shells, crabs, and mollusks. A sinister-looking moray eel peered at us from its hiding place in the shoals near the little dock. We visited other caves where there were Indian writings and hundreds of cave swallows that twittered and flew around our heads when we walked into their domain.

In the evenings we would sit on the beach to watch the sun set and the stars come out. We saw fish-eating bats fish by the light of the moon; we heard the hum of millions of mosquitoes, and noticed the earthy smell of the dew as the night fell around us.

One evening we saw hundreds, yes, hundreds of White-crowned Pigeons flying over our heads in groups of 10 to 15 individuals. They were returning to their *bancos* or roosting areas in the mangroves across the Bay, near Sánchez, after feeding on the wild fruit of the forests of Los Haitises. Toward dusk, as the pigeons flew overhead, we could distinguish their colors with the help of our binoculars, but as it grew darker we could only see large dark birds. When the setting sun reflected on a moving head, however, we could see the white crown tinged with pink in the afterglow. We counted more than a thousand pigeons that passed overhead within an hour.

We were sad when the Orchid Society launch came to pick us up. We had learned a lot, had seen many new things, and had thoroughly enjoyed ourselves in our short sojourn in the miniature paradise of the San Lorenzo Bay.

The Bird with the Foghorn Voice

The Gray-headed Quail Dove

Order:	Columbiformes
Family:	Columbidae
Scientific name:	*Geotrygon caniceps*
English name:	Gray-headed Quail Dove
Spanish name:	Azulona

Of the three Quail Doves that live on the island of Hispaniola, I think the Gray-headed is by far the most beautiful and the rarest. In all the 20 years that I have explored in the mountains of the Dominican Republic, I can count the sightings on the fingers of one hand. However, it may be that the birds are more numerous than we think. They inhabit the highest mountains, in the wildest, most remote areas, and live low down in the underbrush. Therefore they are heard much more than they are seen.

The call is distinctive. A low *"hoo-oop"* is repeated rapidly with a rising inflection, then it changes to a rhythmic throb. It is most disconcerting until the author has been identified as a bird. Many people are afraid of the sound because they think it is the voice of the legendary Ciguapa. The Ciguapa is to the Dominican Republic what Big Foot is to northern California. There are no physical similarities but both are given anthropomorphic qualities. They are never seen, yet there are many people sure of their existence.

The Ciguapa is described as a female, sub-human being about three feet in height, with feet that are fastened on backward. She has long, silky black hair that hangs down to her knees.

There are many stories about how the Ciguapa prowls around looking for victims. She is believed capable of carrying off young children and falling in love with young men. If she happens to become enamoured of a youth who is married, she will get rid of the wife in order to have the husband for herself.

Early one spring day, in the vicinity of "Siberia," a very cold area on a mountainside near Constanza, two pale boys, out of breath from running uphill, came to our camp for help. They had been working in their cabbage patch when they heard strange sounds coming from the bushes. They were sure that a Ciguapa had come to carry them off. They asked my husband to come with his gun.

My husband, always ready to investigate sounds, grabbed the tape recorder.

I knew I would not be welcome in this group, so I prudently didn't ask to go. But as they were leaving, I suggested to my husband that he take the air rifle, too.

"I have a feeling it is an animal of some kind, or even a bird. But the boys will feel more secure if they see you carrying the gun."

So he took the tape recorder and the gun and went with the boys.

He reappeared about an hour later. He began by saying, "I saw the most beautiful pigeon walking about on the ground. I couldn't bear to shoot it!"

How could I mistake its identity after listening to his vivid, accurate description? "The dark plumage of the bird makes it difficult to see as it wanders in and out of the thick foliage. First you see the white forehead, then as it moves the rest of the form comes into focus. What a beautiful combination of variegated color! The head and the upper parts are gray, the upper back is an intense royal purple, the rump is royal blue. The upper breast is tawny, the posterior part of the underpart is rufous. There is some rufous on the wing." Oh, how I wished I had gone down the hill with them! "Never mind," he said. "You can hear the vocalization. I have proved to the boys that it was a bird and not a Ciguapa." Then he played the tape. No wonder the people are afraid when they hear it. The particularly vibrant, loud *hoo-oop* is enough to frighten anyone.

We have heard the Gray-headed Quail dove sing in the Sierra de Neiba, in the Sierra de Baoruco, and in the Cordillera Central, the three principal mountain ranges of the island. I have observed two walking under a giant strangler fig tree on a mountain known as the Nalga de Maco, near the Haitian border. More recently I observed an Azulona on the Casabito Mountain in the Cordillera Central, sitting out a torrential downpour under the broad leaves of a tropical plant. It sat perfectly still for almost 15 minutes, just about five feet from where I stood observing it from under my dripping umbrella.

R. H. Beck, ornithologist and collector for the Smithsonian Institution, discovered this "Blue Pigeon" new to science on the south side of the Cordillera Central, north of Azua, in August, 1916. The ground cover of our mountain ranges has changed so drastically over the years, due to fires, hurricane damage and too much cutting of the forests, that it is a wonder any of these extraordinarily beautiful quail doves have been able to survive.

Very recently a young man who is involved in the government's reforestation program in the Cordillera Central, where the Gray-headed quail dove used to be common, told me that he was having trouble with getting the seeds of the very valuable Green Ebony tree to germinate. This species has been long gone from that area. "What kind of seeds does the Green Ebony produce?" I asked. "They are small, and very, very hard," was the reply. Immediately I thought of the story of the Dodo and the seeds from the *Calvaria mayor*. I wondered if history was repeating itself on another island, half a world away. Is the Quail Dove an intermediate agent that makes for the germination of the Green Ebony seeds, the way the Dodo was for the *Calvaria mayor*?

After hearing the story, the young man is planning to experiment. I most certainly hope that he will be successful!

UPDATE

Milcio Mejías from the Jardín Botánico Nacional executed a project gathering seeds from the bird excreta found under the Ebony tree. He planted them and the seeds germinated. They were on exhibition recently in a Fair in the Botanical Garden.

Polly Parrot Becomes Cuca, La Cotorra

The Hispaniolan Parrot

Order:	Psittaciformes
Family:	Psittacidae
Scientific name:	*Amazona ventralis*
English name:	Hispaniolan Parrot
Spanish name:	Cotorra

Once common, our Hispaniolan Parrot is now on the international list of Endangered Birds. For years and years its habitat has been destroyed as the human population of our island has increased. The forests have been cut and burned, thus doing away with food supplies and nesting sites. As a result, the parrots have developed a taste for plantains, pigeon peas and corn, an appetite which has caused them to be targets for persecution. Many people have used the destruction of crops as an excuse to shoot them and use them for food. Then, to make matters worse, the latest fad of having a parrot for a pet has given the conservationists of the Dominican Republic more cause for worry. The increase in nest robbing for commercial purposes has indeed become a serious problem.

Because of the geographical nature of the island, we have many different kinds of environments. Our parrot has adapted to living in every one of them, from the high mountains to below sea level. Its diet is well varied: it consumes the fruit and seeds of the guayaba, wild figs, wild oranges, cactus and other plants that are plentiful and widely distributed. (The liking for pigeon peas, plantains, and corn has been added after agriculture was well developed.) As for nesting, the birds will use cavities in almost any kind of tree, and cactus as well. We have even had a report of a pair nesting in a cavity on the face of a cliff.

This adaptability has made the Hispaniolan Parrot a highly desired cage bird. It breeds readily in captivity, and for that reason it has been used as a surrogate parent in the program for saving the nearly extinct, closely related Puerto Rican Parrot, *Amazona vittata*.

In the wild the Hispaniolan Parrots are very gregarious and social. They live in bands for most of the year, searching for food together and eating together. At sundown they all fly together to their sleeping tree, and leave together the following day. They converse a great deal while feeding, and squawk and call while flying. I am convinced that, while they feed, they use a sentinel system. If an intruder appears, or if there is danger present, one bird gives a warning call, and suddenly the flock seems to disappear. Their beautiful green coloring gives them a perfect camouflage.

The life history of the parrot is most interesting. They choose mates for life. The mating season lasts for several weeks and a number of maneuvers are involved. First, the two separate from the flock and go off together, hunting or flying or resting quietly on a dead limb in the sun. There is a great deal of chasing, courtship feeding, preening, and even "singing," which at times can be perfectly ludicrous. It seems that the birds want to sing of their love and affection, but nothing comes out except a few loud croaks and squawks.

Once, early in March, we were camped on the north side of the mountain "204" in the Nelba range, at an elevation of about 5,000 feet. That particular part of the mountain had been logged off except for some big trees that were growing in the ravines. Bracken ferns, low brush and grasses covered the mountainside, while on the east side of the International Highway where we made camp there was an elfin forest of virgin vegetation that was wonderful to behold.

From that patch of trees came a chorus of bird songs that was thrilling beyond words. The boom of the Gray-headed Quail Dove and the cardinal-like song of the Chat Tanager stood out above all else. The chattering trill of the Hispaniolan Siskin and the *"Wis-wis-wis-wis"* of the Constanza Sparrow came from the hillsides. The Striped-headed Tanager and the Greater Antillean Bullfinches flew in and out. I could see some singing, but the songs of both of these latter species are so high-pitched it is most difficult to hear them.

Out of all this activity, about 8 a.m. a pair of parrots flew over the elfin forest and came to rest on an exposed branch of a dead tree very close to our camp. The sexes are so very similar I couldn't tell the differences between them, even though I was close enough to see them in every detail.

I had a ringside seat at a beautiful performance.

For a while the two birds sat separately and preened. Then one went to sit closer to the other, clucking and making other squawky noises. There was considerable pecking and feeding motions, then one flew to a higher branch and sang. I detected a particular rhythm that could have been called a primitive melody. After the serenade, the pair flew away together.

Later in the courtship period, the pair choose a territory. They are vicious if there are intruders. We have seen some birds fight to exhaustion. One biologist reported that he saw such a terrific fight that the vanquished one lost an eye.

The parrots make a good deal of fuss over choosing their nesting site. When all is arranged to the satisfaction of the female, two or three white eggs are laid. The male assists in the work of incubation, sometimes feeding the incubating female. Incubation lasts for 27 to 28 days. When the babies emerge from the shell they are naked and blind. They look like little old men in miniature. The young ones are fed from the parent's craw until they fledge. There is a high mortality rate among the parrot young. They do not become sexually mature until three years of age.

After the young are fledged, the family joins the flock to participate in group activity.

The Hispaniolan Parrot is about 11-12 inches in length. It is bright green on the upper parts; the lower parts are green with a browning-red spot on the lower breast. The posterior parts are bright yellow. The wings are bright blue underneath; there is a white spot on the forehead and just above the beak. A black spot adorns the cheek.

Although our parrots are rapidly decreasing, in spite of the campaign for their protection, the Dominican Republic has a better population of native parrots than any other of the islands in the Caribbean. They would have a much better chance to survive if the hunting and commercialization could be more effectively controlled.

The Termite Nest is Home to the Parakeet

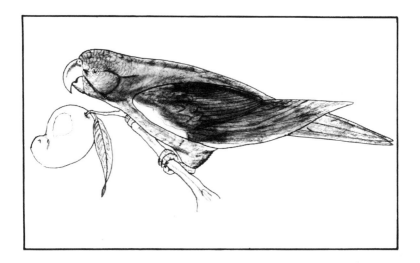

The Hispaniolan Parakeet

Order:	Psittaciformes
Family:	Psittacidae
Scientific name:	*Aratinga chloroptera*
English name:	Hispaniolan Parakeet
Spanish name:	Perico

It is a most interesting experience to see a flock of Hispaniolan Parakeets disappear like magic in front of your eyes. First you see them, then you don't. A group of a hundred individuals can disappear without making a bit of noise and without your seeing them go. They just blend in with the foliage and become invisible. The beautiful bright green coloring of the Parakeet is protective. Only a spot or two of red on the breast shows up when the bird is at rest. But what a brilliant sight it is to see a flock wheel and turn together in flight, when the striking red of the underwings flashes in the sun!

Late one afternoon near Monteada Nueva, in the Sierra de Baorurco, we walked up the side of a hill where we could see down into a deep canyon. Right below us, beside the road that wound through an ancient stream bed, grew a huge strangler fig tree. The tree was laden with yellow fruit that contrasted sharply with the broad, glossy green leaves. As I contemplated the scene, I heard screeches and suddenly a great flock of parakeets appeared and landed in the tree. What a racket! They pushed and shoved and vied for the best places to eat, then finally settled down to feed. I wondered how many birds were in the flock.

I focused my binoculars and tried to count, but had no luck because the leaves and the birds seemed to be a moving sea of green. I tried to estimate numbers but just then I sneezed! One bird gave a peculiar call and they were all gone, just like that. I didn't see a bird fly. They just quietly moved back of the leaves and became silent. They were part of the tree.

Our beautiful Parakeets are fast becoming rare. Since colonial times the forests have been slashed and burned for agricultural purposes until there is not much left of the Parakeet's natural wild food supply. As a result, the birds have developed a hearty appetite for some of the garden stuff, such as pigeon peas and corn on the cob. Consequently the farmers consider them pests that should be eliminated. In many regions they are used as food.

The *Aratinga chloroptera* lives in the same habitat as the Hispaniolan Parrot, with preference for the mountain woodlands. Their eating and nesting habits are similar, but at times the Parakeets will nest in abandoned termite constructions instead of in a tree cavity. Two to six white eggs are laid.

Some people have trouble distinguishing the Hispaniolan Parakeet from the Hispaniolan Parrot because of their color. Close observance will show that the Parakeet is much slimmer than the Parrot, and it has a long pointed tail, whereas the Parrot is stocky, with a short square tail. When flying the Parakeets go in a direct line, using strong wing beats that make for rapid flight. The Parrot's flight is weak and with short wing beats. At times it seems that they have trouble in staying aloft. The vocalizations are easily distinguished. Parakeets screech and Parrots squawk.

In the Dominican Republic the Parakeet is found throughout the island. Until 1970 a few small flocks could be observed on the southwestern side of the city of Santo Domingo.

Apparently the Parakeet used to live on Mona Island and in Puerto Rico, but it has been considered extinct in that area since 1892. However, recent reports inform us that several pairs have been found nesting in Puerto Rico and in Florida. It is reasonable to suggest that these birds are escapees, and since the climate of Puerto Rico and Florida is very much like that of the Dominican Republic, it was not difficult for the Parakeets to become adapted.

A Very Deceitful Bird

The Bay-breasted Cuckoo

Order:	Cuculiformes
Family:	Cuculidae
Scientific name:	*Hyetornis rufigularis*
English name:	Bay-breasted Cuckoo
Spanish name:	Tacot, Cúa

The Hispaniolan Bay-breasted Cuckoo, *Hyetornis rufigularis*, is described by Wetmore in Bulletin #155 of the Smithsonian Institution (1931) as "resident, locally common." Judging from the number of specimens taken up to 1927, one can really believe the report. The Smithsonian alone had 17 specimens and the Tring

Museum had seven, all taken from the same general area of the Cordillera Central: Honduras, Loma Tina, Constanza, Miranda, La Vega, Tubano, and San José de Ocoa. I have never seen the bird in any of those locations but I have had three sightings in Valdesia, which is found on the south side of the eastern extreme of the same mountain range. According to my field notes, my first sighting occurred in April, 1971; the other two were reported in the 1981 and 1982 Christmas Bird Counts.

The years were long and many before we could say we had actually seen and heard the Bay-breasted Cuckoo. We had had fleeting glimpses of it in Bánica and along the Haitian border near Pedro Santana, but we despaired of ever making a study of it. Nevertheless we learned a great deal about the other members of the Cuckoo family.

We learned that the Hispaniolan Lizard Cuckoo is *the* common Cuckoo; it lives everywhere. We learned that the Yellow-billed Cuckoo is called the "Primavera" (Spring) because it "disappears" in December and returns in the spring. Several times when we heard its slow *"Cow, cow, cow, cow"* call, we thought that it might be the Cúa sound. But when we saw the source of the vocalization, we knew we were mistaken.

We learned that the Mangrove Cuckoo lives in other places besides the mangroves and that the Black-billed Cuckoo is transitory. On its return flight to the north in April it is vociferous, and how we do enjoy hearing its peculiar song! We also learned that the Smooth-billed Ani is an aberrant member of the Cuckoo group. We learned to distinguish all the different Cuckoo calls, that is, all but the Bay-breasted Cuckoo. Not only were we frustrated but apprehensive. This bird is found only on Hispaniola. It is endemic to that island. If the number of birds collected by American museums by 1927 was any indication of the existing numbers of the bird, was our inability to find one for study an indication that in less than fifty years it was near extinction?

My first real encounter with the Bay-breasted Cuckoo occurred during Easter week, 1972. We were on the return trip from an orchid-hunting expedition to Loma de Toro, in the Sierra de

Baoruco, when night descended upon us in the flat, dry area below Aguacate, the guard station on the Haitian border. We made our camp close to the "Cruces de Puerto Escondido."

After our week's stay in the cold, high mountains, we noticed the radical change of temperature, and the hordes of mosquitoes that zinged around our heads were very bothersome. Our two guests—Dr. George Reynard of Philadelphia and my husband's brother, Dr. Kenneth S. Dod, from Berkeley, California—were quite uncomfortable in the heat, but we seasoned tropical dwellers welcomed the change.

To accommodate our guests we prepared our camp with haste, putting up the tent first so we could change our heavy clothing for something lighter and daub ourselves with repellent for protection against the biting insects.

Later, as we ate our evening meal, we planned the activities for the following day.

"Let's take advantage of the early morning hours for the birding," said my husband. "Then light out for home before it gets too hot." At that point in time there was no direct road over the hills between Duverge and Puerto Escondido. We had to skirt Lago Enriquillo on the south side, then take off on a long, hard pull over the foothills of the Sierra de Baoruco, across almost impossible roads and steep grades. The drivers of the cars never liked that part of the trip but others on the expedition did! There were always many birds to keep us entertained during the tedious journey.

We birded a while before we retired. We heard a Toríco *(Siphonhoris brewsteri)* singing in the distance, and a Pitanguá gave its plaintive cry. A Barn Owl screeched and George thought he heard a Potoo.

We were awakened early by the sound of rain falling on the metal roof of the van. By daylight, however, the rain had ended and the bird life and the insect population were out in full force. I made coffee and put out the breakfast foods but no one ate. The smell of the moisture on the dry forest and the coolness of the air had sharpened our perceptions. We could move without making any noise and we were hearing and seeing all kinds of things.

We decided to separate: Don left with the air rifle and his tape recorder, George went off in another direction with his recorder, "Dr. Kenny" went his way and I went mine. I saw some interesting migratory warblers, some Pine Siskins out of their normal habitat, the Flat-billed Vireo, and a pair of Piculets. I heard Trogons calling. I wondered what they were doing in the desert. Had they descended to the lower elevations in search of food, or were they residents? Then I heard a most peculiar call. *"Cúa, cúa, cúa"* echoed loud and clear through the woods. I had never heard anything like it before. The Trogons were forgotten, I had to find the source of that wild, harsh sound.

Since I have a hearing problem, I was a bit befuddled. I heard the calls and I heard answers but I could not tell from which direction the sounds were coming. I decided that I'd just stand still and perhaps the creature, whatever it was, would come close enough for me to see it. At that moment I heard the unmistakeable bleat of a small goat in distress. I thought of the story of Moses in the desert. The kid must be caught in a thorn bush, I thought, since most of the vegetation was cactus or bushes with thorns.

Again came the weird *Cúa* cry.

"Maybe it is a disturbed parrot," I guessed. "Whatever it is, it is angry and ready to fight."

I felt something touch my arm and I jumped. It was Dr. Kenny, who had come up behind me. I had been so engrossed in the sounds that I had neither heard nor seen him come.

"What is it?" he whispered. He, too, had heard the strange vocalizations. "Is it a bird, beast, or fish?"

"I don't know," I answered. "Listen!"

The calls were getting closer and louder; it appeared that the sound was coming our way. I saw something move through the low bushes to my left, about ten yards ahead. It was Don with the gun and the recorder. Presently George arrived on the scene. He, too, had followed the sound, but had he and Don been answering each other?

Suddenly a large gray bird with rufous-colored underparts and a long, laddered tail appeared in a moderately tall tree, about 25 yards in front of us. It rested a moment and called *"Cúa."* Then it bleated like a young kid.

No other sound in the world could be like that loud, raucous, explosive call. It was not like the voice of any other cuckoo I had ever heard. No written description by a person who knew the bird could come close to explaining it. Neither George nor Don nor I had been able to guess that we were hearing the Bay-breasted Cuckoo. It was something you comprehended only when you yourself heard it and saw it with your own eyes.

Then came the crack of the air rifle. The bird just sat and gave the Cúa cry again. Again and yet again the shot sounded, but in its own good time the big cuckoo flew back in the direction from which it had come.

"Why did you shoot at it?" I cried. "Oh, why did you shoot?"

"A bird in hand is worth two in the bush," came the reply from my husband. "That is a *Hyetornis rufigularis*, high on your list of priorities."

There was no use lamenting. The bird had flown, and everyone knew that it was senseless to try to follow a cuckoo through a forest. Everyone, that is, except my brother-in-law, who started off at a dog-trot and was gone for over an hour.

George, Don, and I went back to the car to get ready for the return trip to the capital. We ate and had piled the last of our gear into the van when Kenny showed up, hot, sweaty, and covered with burrs and spines from the cactus and other desert plants. He held his hands behind his back, and had a sort of crooked grin on his face.

"Guess what I found," he said.

"An orchid?" asked my husband.

"A bird's nest?" asked George.

Before I could make my guess, and with a great flourish and a wide smile, Dr. Kenny spread out his hands and showed us a beautiful specimen of the Bay-breasted Cuckoo. We could not find a visible wound any place on its body but it was dead.

"How did you find it?" I asked, incredulous.

"Well, I followed it because I noticed that it was descending as it flew. I followed until it hit the ground, behind a bush, then I lost track. I must have searched under every bush or tree and in between, in a radius of over 100 yards. I was about to give up when I spotted it in plain sight. That gray color of the upper parts looks just like the dirt!"

And that was how we got our first and only skin of the *Hyetornis rufigularis*. When we examined the body in the lab, we found it to be a female. There were some remains of an insect and two small lizards in the stomach. We also found that the windpipe had been cleanly severed. Don's aim had been better than we thought.

For several years we looked for the nest of this rare bird in the vicinity of Puerto Escondido, but were never successful in finding it. We found a place outside of La Descubierta near the Lago Enriquillo, where there was a population and we'd show them off to our visitors. That wooded area no longer exists.

In April, 1983, my luck changed. I found a place where the Bay-breasted Cuckoo is common. With the help of a guide, I found three nests.

Near a little village about an hour's ride from Loma Cabrera, called Rió Limpio, the birds were seen frequently in yards and gardens. Their strange cries echo through the valleys and on the hillsides. It is *the* common cuckoo and it is respected as being a beneficial bird. It is called the "Cúa" because of its peculiar hoarse and explosive call.

The nest of the Cúa is to be found in almost any kind of tree that has epiphytes or leaves that will conceal the construction. It is a platform of twigs, filled in and shaped with leaves, placed about 20-25 feet from the ground. There were incubating birds on two of the nests we found, but the third one looked as if it had been disturbed. We never were able to see directly into the nests to check the number or the color of the eggs, but the guide said that two white eggs are laid.

I am planning a return trip to Rio Limpio for next April. I'd like to make some further bird studies there. I'd spy on the Bay-breasted Cuckoo and look for the caves where the Ashy-faced

Barn Owl lives. I'd like to find out if the Common Yellowthroat makes a nest in the bog where I saw a female carrying dry grass in her beak. I'd try to get some photographs of the Trogons that live only a half-hour's walk up the Arbitonito River, where the virgin forest is.

Wouldn't you like to join me?

The Cuckoo that Isn't Crazy

The Hispaniolan Lizard Cuckoo

Order:	Cuculiformes
Family:	Cuculidae
Scientific name:	*Saurothera longirostris*
English name:	Hispaniolan Lizard Cuckoo
Spanish:	Pájaro Bobo

When translated into English, the words "Pájaro Bobo" mean "Foolish Bird." Our *Saurothera longirostris* is a long way from being foolish, although you have to admit that at times it certainly seems that way.

The very common Pájaro Bobo is a rather tame bird that seems to have an insatiable curiosity. Look for the bird and you will probably find it looking at you. It cranes its neck and moves its head from side to side to get a better view. When it finally realizes it has been discovered, it literally runs through the leafy trees, jumping from one branch to another until it disappears right in front of your eyes, leaving you to feel like the foolish one. The Pájaro Bobo is high on my list of beautiful birds. The warm brown of the upper parts contrasts well with the light orange spot under the chin, and the two-tone brick color of the underparts makes it a symphony of colors. To set it apart from all the other species of this family on Hispaniola, the *Saurothera longirostris* has a patch of bright red, bare, skin around its eyes, making it almost impossible to mistake its identity.

Our "cuckoo," like all other New World cuckoos, makes its own rustic nest, which it cleverly conceals in bromeliads, leafy trees or dry, dead branches about eight to ten feet from the ground. Two medium-size white eggs are laid. Since the sexes are similar, it is difficult to tell whether or not the work of procreation is shared by the two sexes.

Their diet is composed of caterpillars, small mice, and smallish lizards. They are considered most beneficial by the farmers, particularly by those who raise tobacco.

Even though the birds are beneficial, they are used for food. Many people believe that the flesh has medicinal value and will improve the appetite of a sickly child.

My first experience with the Pájaro Bobo led us far afield from our original plans. It was a memorable experience, even though we felt frustrated as well as humiliated. We had to travel 50 extra miles, we lost prime time for recording bird songs, and we were treated like delinquent children.

Dr. George B. Reynard, the plant geneticist and ornithologist specializing in the recording of bird songs, had arrived in the country on a routine visit to the tomato plantations. Due to adverse weather conditions, he finished his work a day ahead of schedule and wanted to take advantage of his extra time. My husband planned a trip to Casabito, in the district of La Vega, where in 1970 there was a goodly portion of broadleaf rain forest. Since it is only a two-hour drive from Santo Domingo, we thought we could start early, take lunch along, and work all day.

At the last minute my husband could not go.

"There is no reason why you two have to stay home," he said emphatically. "Get up early, take the VW, and go as planned. You know the road, Tudy, it isn't all that complicated. And George, you've had experience with a VW bus. The roads are good. Go on."

So we did. We left the house about 4 a.m. to arrive at the crest of Casabito at daybreak. We had no trouble finding a parking spot at the right of the entrance to the old logging road. We gathered up our recording equipment, our binoculars, locked the car, and started out.

What a chorus of bird songs greeted us! It was April and every bird was declaring its territory. The Constanza Sparrow trilled from a dead branch of an old pine tree. Some squawking parrots flew by, a noisy band of Palm Crows discovered us, and the famous Solitaire was tuning up his Solitaire whistle. Trogons were calling from every side and some parakeets were screeching from the canyon below. What a beautiful day for recording! No wind, no car noises, no dogs barking, and no burros braying!

We walked and worked along the old logging road for almost two hours before we felt hungry enough to start back for lunch. On the way back we found a Pájaro Bobo so close to us and so vociferous that we knew we were close to a nest. We were able to record many vocalizations.

Finally we arrived in sight of the car where, to our surprise, we found two men dressed in military attire, holding machine guns.

George, not knowing Spanish, told me I would have to do the talking. "But don't make them angry. Remember, they have the guns."

"We haven't done anything wrong to be arrested for," I replied. "I'm not afraid of them. But I promise not to do anything rash."

I greeted them pleasantly, with a hearty "Buenos días, amigos. ¿Qué podemos hacer para servirles?" (Good morning, friends. What may we do to serve you?)

"We have orders to take you to the Commander in Constanza."

"Why, señores? We were working here on an important project and if we are taken to Constanza we will lose our good morning hours, when it is the best time to work."

"What are you doing here?"

"We are recording bird songs to make a record. Would you like to hear some?"

"Yes, indeed," said the younger man, and we played our recordings of the morning. Reluctantly the older man admitted that we had good recordings, but that didn't really explain what we were doing there.

"You are outsiders," he said. "What are you doing on state land?"

"Just what I told you. We want to make a record of our bird songs."

"You can record bird songs anywhere. Why did you come up here?"

"I told you already, Sr., that we know this area. My husband and I have been up here before to record bird songs."

"Does your husband speak Spanish?"

"Yes, Sr., fluently."

"Then this man is not your husband. He doesn't know Spanish at all. Why are you up here with a man who is not your husband?"

I tried to explain, but the man refused to listen. I could feel my control slipping away. Imagine accusing me of being unfaithful to my husband! But that was beside the point, I thought. Is he just trying to make me mad?

"I have permission from my husband to be here! It makes no difference if my friend is not my husband. I am doing scientific research and I have permission as a resident of this country to go wherever I want. Why are you arresting us?"

George said, "Don't argue any more. It won't help. Let them take us to Constanza."

"But we'll lose the entire day!"

"Let's not have any trouble," he said with resignation. "We'll have another chance."

So we drove the 25 miles to Constanza with the two men with machine-guns in the back seat.

The commander of the outpost kept us waiting for almost half an hour before he finally called us into his office.

I explained to him what we were doing and why. "You were on dangerous ground, Doña!"

"Why is it dangerous ground? There are no wild animals there, there are no thieves or bad people in the country. Why do you call it dangerous?"

"It is state land! I saw your minibus parked there, abandoned, and I wanted to know what you were doing there."

"I have a right to go on state land. I have permission as a resident of the Dominican Republic. There are no signs that say that Casabito is off-limits!"

He did not want to pursue the subject and since he realized I was not to be intimidated, he decided to let well enough alone. He offered us some coffee, changed the subject, then told us to go home. I thanked him and told him it was nice to know that the lands of the state were so closely guarded and protected.

What irony! A few months later I related my experience to a friend who was working in the Department of Forestry and he told us why we had been arrested.

We had been arrested because we were too close to a clandestine operation! The same commander was taking out green ebony trees on land that belonged to the state! The officer had been found out and demoted.

The recordings of the *Saurothera longirostris* that we made that morning were so good that they were selected to appear on the record, making our unexpected aggravation easy to forget.

A Devil in Bird's Feathers

The Stygian Owl

Order:	Strigiformes
Family:	Strigidae
Scientific name:	*Asio stygius noctipetens*
English name:	Stygian Owl, Devil Owl
Spanish name:	Ciguapa, Lechuza Orejita

The Stygian Owl was known on the island of Quisqueya long before Columbus discovered the New World. A carved wooden figure of a bird with ear tufts found in a cave and an Indian drawing on a cave wall indicate that this owl could have been a important part of an ancient religious ritual or that it was a familiar figure in the caves where the Indians sought refuge.

Apparently this bird was known to Vieillot, who did some scientific studies in Haiti in 1807 (Bulletin #155, Smithsonian Institution, 1933, pp. 245-247). He used the name "Bubo clamator" and said the inhabitants knew of an owl that was called the "Houhou."

Asio stygius is about 15-17 inches in length. It is a very dark brown "long-eared" owl, with a dark facial disk, the upperparts mottled with buffy, heavily streaked and barred with black or dark brown, becoming paler on the lower abdomen. The ear tufts or "horns" are dark brown. The legs and toes are feathered (Peterson and Chalif, in *A Field Guide to Mexican Birds*, say "feet naked, eyes yellow").

The Hispaniolan race of the Stygian Owl *(Asio stygius noctipetens)* is one of six subspecies of this forest-dwelling species whose range includes Mexico, Nicaragua (two races), and Cuba including the Isle of Pines, with a possible disjunct population in Brazil, Paraguay and Argentina. It is, in turn, one of six members of the genus *Asio* which includes our Long-eared and Short-eared Owls, two owls from Africa and one from Madagascar.

Asio stygius noctipetens Riley is listed by Alexander Wetmore in Bulletin 155 of the Smithsonian as a rare resident of the Dominican Republic. I quote: "Little is at present known of this owl, first described from an adult male secured by Dr. W. L. Abbott near Constanza at an elevation of about 1200 meters. September 23, 1916. Kaempfer collected a second bird from the swampy forests at the mouth of the Río Yuna, which Hartert said is an adult female, taken November 18, 1922. Ciffere secured skins at Moca January 1, 1927 and July 6, 1919."

It is the author's opinion that the status of the Stygian Owl has not changed since that bulletin was issued. I know of only three confirmed sightings and one collected specimen between the years 1929 and 1977. They are as follows: George B. Reynard and the author saw one at the mouth of a cave located close to Ensanche Alma Rosa, at the eastern edge of Santo Domingo in November,

1970. John Terbrough's group of students from Princeton University reported one near Jarabacoa in a pine forest during the first week of February, 1973 (personal communication). Jim and Beth Wiley, ornithologists from Puerto Rico, flushed one in Los Naranjos, near Puerto Escondido in April, 1976 (personal communication). And as a result of publicity provided by the author, a specimen, badly mounted and with no date whatsoever, was brought to the Museo Nacional de Historia Natural during the last week of April, 1977. The specimen had recently been taken in an old, abandoned cacao plantation close to the mouth of the Río Yuna. With the arrival of the mounted bird, we knew for certain that the Stygian Owl still existed on the island.

A sighting in April, 1978, resulting in a complete set of vocal recordings and some unsatisfactory photographs, was the culmination of eight years of intensive work on the part of George B. Reynard, Donald D. Dod and the author. We had some interesting adventures; some were discouraging and disappointing; others were frightening; some were fun. We slept in caves, hiked for miles and suffered many insect bites. We sweltered in the lowlands and shivered in the frosty nights up in the mountains. We saw some beautiful country and became acquainted with many *campesinos* who were interested in our investigations. They gave us much reliable and valuable information.

This owl has many vernacular names: Cu-chi, Ciguapa, Hu-hu, and La Lechuza Orejita. In English the bird is often called the Devil Owl.

One important bit of information eventually led us to discover the bird. We learned from the inhabitants of Los Haitises that the Stygian Owl is generally silent, giving only one loud "Hu" once in a while, emitted sometime around midnight. However, during the breeding season, apparently during the months of November, February, and April, the male calls with low-pitched *"hoos"* and the female answer with higher-pitched whistles or screams, and they respond antiphonally at short intervals. We heard the male call several times before we were lucky enough to record the antiphonal performance.

We set up our camps in many places: Constanza, Jarabacoa, Bayajibe, Monte Plata, Pilancón, Boca de Yuma, and several sites between Sabana de la Mar and Miches, Hoyoncito and Arroyon. We maintained nocturnal vigilance, alternating watches, from early evening until dawn. Finally in April, 1978, at Pumosen, in a virgin forest, a three hour's walk from the end of the road, we succeeded in obtaining photographs and recordings. (Record: "Bird Songs in the Dominican Republic/Cantos de Aves en la República Dominicana." George B. Reynard with the assistance of Donald D. and Annabelle Dod. Published by Cornell University Laboratory of Ornithology, October, 1981.)

A youth from Hoyoncito showed me an old nest in a cana palm *(Sabal umbraculifera)* that was probably the nest of the Stygian Owl. It was largely composed of grasses, placed loosely together, about 15-20 feet from the ground. He told me there had been two nestlings.

Although we were not able to make a biological study of the Stygian Owl, we have discovered some reasons for its scarcity. This rare bird seems to be known in the Dominican Republic only where virgin forests still exist. All recent sightings have occurred in old forests, sometimes near caves but never near houses or in second-growth trees. We also learned that the Stygian Owl is better known in the northeastern part of the island, where the karst limestone hills limit the destruction of the forests.

Since the time when the first Spanish colonists arrived on the island in 1493 there has been a continuous destruction of the forests. This may have contributed to the extirpation of several small mammals (José Alberto Ottenwalder, personal communication). (The later introduction of the destructive, carnivorous mongoose could have also contributed to their demise.) Although we have no proof, it is easy to believe that these small mammals which no longer exist were an important part of the owl's food supply. Loss of both habitat and the source of food certainly must have caused a notable decline in the numbers of the Stygian Owl.

Fear of the bird is another reason for its scarcity. The Stygian Owl is associated with the devil because of its ear tufts. It is considered to have supernatural powers. One belief is that it can transform itself from a bird into a witch; as a witch it is believed to suck the blood of unbaptized children. As a result of such superstitions, the owl is considered an enemy—one to be feared and eliminated if at all possible.

Additionally, hunting was a very popular sport in Hispaniola during colonial times and some of that old culture survives today. Every boy who is big enough to walk has a slingshot, and the youth who can afford it has a shotgun or an air rifle. Often military personnel use birds as targets, to improve their aim, and sportsmen consider hunting the best of pastimes. A bird as big as the Stygian owl doesn't have a chance if hunting is not controlled.

The owl is very vulnerable. Its habit of shrinking down and making itself as small as possible, and then hiding close to the tree trunk instead of flying when discovered, makes it an easy mark for a slingshot, a gun or even a thrown stone.

Because of the remoteness and the inaccessibility of the national parks that are found in the Cordillera Central, we have not been able to ascertain the presence of the Stygian Owl in those areas. However, it is very gratifying to know that the territory of two recently-created national parks extends into the areas where we know there are small populations of this rare bird. It has been seen in a cave in the Parque del Este and heard in the interior of the Parque de Los Haitises, in an area known as Monte Bonito. With the protection offered by the parks system and an educational program, it may have a better chance to increase in number. But until its populations increase, *Asio stygius* must be considered one of our rarest and most endangered species.

I wish to thank my husband Donald D. Dod for his helpful and constructive criticisms in the preparation of this paper. I also wish to thank José Alberto Ottenwalder, zoologist at the Museo Nacional de Historia Natural de Santo Domingo.

A Witch That Flies on Wings, Not a Broomstick

The Potoo

Order:	Caprimulgiformes
Family:	Nyctibiidae
Scientific name:	*Nyctibius jamaicensis* *(abbottii?)*
English name:	Potoo
Spanish name:	Don Juan, Bruja, Lechusa, Chat Huant (Haiti)

The Potoo was first discovered on the Island of Hispaniola in Haiti. W.L. Abbott secured a specimen of what was thought to be *Nyctibius griseus* on March 9, 1917. It was taken alive while asleep. On February 12, 1918, Abbott wrote from Jeremie that he had heard many "Chat Huants" but he was not able to obtain another specimen. On May 20, 1920, the bird was reported from the Cul de Sac region. On June 28, 1918, James Bond collected a female on Gonâve, taking it from Pointe-à-Raquette. The body was preserved in alcohol, and Dr. Alexander Wetmore from the Smithsonian Institution published an account of the anatomy.

In the Dominican Republic, Abbott examined a Potoo, badly mounted, in a drugstore in Puerto Plata. He also reported hearing the bird give a weird vocalization near "Hondo" and had reports from *campesinos* that it lived in San Francisco de Macoris. Hartert reported a specimen in Tring Museum, taken by Kaempfer near Tubano (Padre Las Casas) in October, 1923.

None of the visiting ornithologists had ever seen the Potoo alive in the Dominican Republic. We, too, had never seen it, but we were determined to find it. We used the illustrations from James Bond's book *Birds of the West Indies*, and George Reynard obtained a tape recording of the vocalization of *Nyctibius jamaicensis* from Jamaica.

We carried this material in the camper and everywhere we went we asked questions. We learned many superstitions, a great deal of folklore, and some incredible stories as well as some credible ones. We learned that the bird is known by several names. In the South it is called "Lechusa" (Owl); in the Cibao it is called Bruja (Witch); and in the East it is called the Don Juan Grande.

Once, while camping in Palma Dulce, near Duverge, we met some *campesinos* who were working on an irrigation project. When we showed them our picture, one man named Sandino said, "Oh, I know that bird! About two weeks ago, while I was cutting a tree right over there, a big, dark bird fell out of the branches and hit the ground. It was stunned for a minute, but not hurt. I tried to catch it because it appeared to have good meat for eating, but before I could reach it, it flew to a low branch. I had a good chance to see it."

"It had a short beak and a wide, ugly mouth. Why, that mouth was so big it looked like it could swallow a mango! Its eyes were shut, the tail was long, and it had dark and light feathers all mixed together. I said, 'Ay, Virgen de la Altagracia, what kind of a bird can this ugly thing be? I'm going to kill it!'

"But do you know, I threw five stones and I couldn't hit it although it was very close and I'm not a bad shot, either. So I said, 'Ugly bird, you must be protected by God and the Virgin of High Grace. Go in peace, because I won't throw stones at you any more. It finally flew a little way because it appeared to be blind in the daylight."

The other workers on the project verified Sandino's story. They also said they had not seen the strange bird from that day on.

After many long, interesting but difficult trips in search of the Potoo, we discovered a charcoal maker on the south side of the island in the little town of Enriquillo. He said he was working in the dry forest near the foothills when he discovered a strange bird that had the face of an owl and a long tail, nesting on the stub of an old tree. He told us that there was only one white egg and the adult bird incubated it standing upright, holding the egg between its feet. He said the bird looked like a piece of the stub, a continuation of the dead tree. He observed it often; it was a long time before the egg hatched. When the *pichon* (nestling) finally came out of the shell, its claws were well developed because it clung to the stump. It took a long time for the little one to fly away.

One brilliant moonlight night in April, 1973, we camped again near the irrigation project (now finished) in Palma Dulce. Our friend, George Reynard, who was with us, slept on a cot by the side of the car so he could hear the calls of the night birds. About 1:30 a.m. George woke us up, saying "Listen, listen! I hear the Potoo calling."

It didn't take us long to wake up. Oh, what a voice! "Kwah, waugh, waugh, waugh, kwaah!" it said, sounding like a devil laughing from the shadows. No wonder the country people call it a witch and are afraid of it!

We recorded the sounds, then we set forth to find the bird, playing the tapes and then listening for answers. Oh, what fun we had trekking through an unknown dry forest by the light of the moon, trying to move in the direction from which the sounds were coming! We found a clear spot among trees at the edge of a plantation of plantains, where a burro corral was located. Suddenly a large bird flew out of the shadows and hovered over the head of George, who was carrying the tape recorder. The Potoo was challenging an intruder in its territory. We had luck at last!

We spent the rest of the night following the Potoo from one post to another. The yellow eyes were like big beacons when they reflected the light from our flashlights. It hawked for insects, then would return to a perch, much after the fashion of flycatchers.

Two years later we managed to take a specimen from this area for the scientific collection of the National Museum of Natural History in Santo Domingo.

In subsequent investigations we have found small populations of the Potoo in other areas of the south: Puerto Escondido, Barahona, and La Descubierta as well as in the interior of the eastern part of the island: Hoyón, Almirante, and near Hato Mayor.

The Potoo is generally found in or around animal corrals. Its principal food is the dung beetle. Like other members of this order, the potoo flies through the air at night with its mouth open to capture its nocturnal prey.

Because of the tape recordings and other studies, it has been learned that there are differences between our potoo and the one from Jamaica, and that the Jamaican Potoo is not *Nyctibius griseus*, as was once thought. Until investigations are complete, we will not know just where the potoo will be placed. Whatever it is, we know it is a very intriguing bird, beneficial, beautiful, and rare. Lucky is the person who has the privilege of seeing or hearing one!

He Sings His Own Name in Spanish

The Least Pauraque

Order:	Caprimulgiformes
Family:	Caprimulgidae
Scientific name:	*Siphonorhis brewsteri*
English name:	Least Pauraque
Spanish name:	El Torico

The Least Pauraque of Hispaniola has been known to science for 62 years. Rollo H. Beck collected the first specimen at Tubano (now known as Padre Las Casas) near Azua in the Dominican Republic on February 10, 1917 (Beck, 1921). The specimen was described by Frank Chapman with the name *Microsiphonorhis brewsteri* that same year (Chapman, 1917). In 1924, E. Kaempfer also took three specimens near Tubano (Wetmore and Swales,

1931). In Haiti the Least Pauraque was first identified from bones in cave deposits at L'Atalaye (Wetmore and Swales, *ibid)*. In 1928, James Bond assigned the species to the genus *Siphonorhis* (Bond, 1928).

In a letter to me dated September 13, 1982, James Bond related, "In 1928 I collected a series of this species on Gonâve Island in addition to young and sets of eggs...I encountered many Greater Antillean Nightjars in Cuba and collected a set of eggs of this Caprimulgid on the Isle of Pines, but I heard this bird only once in Haiti, at an arid locality called Magasin Caries between Port-au-Prince and St. Marc. The Least Pauraque was there also."

I know of no other reports of the Least Pauraque from the Dominican Republic or Haiti between 1928 and 1969. Albert Schwartz of the Miami-Dade Community College, Florida, who has done extensive field work in the Dominican Republic from 1950 to 1977 in the disciplines of herpetology and ornithology, states in a letter of October 7, 1977, that "I know of no one other than myself and my parties who have worked in the Dominican Republic in the time span that you mention." He continued in another letter, "I have neither collected *Siphonorhis* nor any other *Caprimulgus* in either [the Dominican Republic or Haiti], nor even in the places where Dr. Bond found them common in Haiti."

Charles Wood of the Department of Zoology, University of Vermont, worked on wintering warblers in southwestern Haiti from 1974 through 1977. On November 21, 1977, he told me that he did not hear, see, or collect any *Caprimulgides* in Haiti in that period.

In 1971, in the 14th supplement to Birds of the West Indies, Bond makes this note: "*Siphonorhis brewsteri*: Tape recordings of the voice obtained by George Reynard in a semi-arid region about 20 kilometers south of Monte-Cristi bordering on the Copey-Pepillo-Salcedo road." The date of this recording was March 29, 1969. This appears to be the first report of the existence of the endemic Least Pauraque of Hispaniola in 41 years.

My first contact with *S. brewsteri* occurred in August, 1971, when my husband and I were camping near Galindo, a small village in the Sierra de Martin Garcia, to the south of Azua and only about 25 miles from Padre Las Casas. At eventide at our camp, we heard a strange call, perhaps best rendered orthographically as *"To-rí-co, to-rí-co, to-rí-co."* Never having heard this sound before, we recorded it. In the early morning, another call, a clear, rising whistle woke us, and in the light of a late moon we looked for the maker of the song. We saw something that flew like a giant moth, erratic and floppy, moving between the trees. That same morning, when charcoal makers working near our campsite arrived, they identified the singer as the "Toríco" and described the bird so vividly that we had no difficulty in identifying it as the Least Pauraque. We had stumbled on another population of the unreported *S. brewsteri*!

After that trip we discovered the "Toríco" in many different areas and were able to collect a specimen on the Mota Farm in Jarabacoa in April, 1975. The bird, a male, measured 203.1 mm long, the tail 107.6 mm, the bend of the wing to primaries 116.0 mm, and the culmen to base 10.7 mm. It is rufous-browning gray above, with a mottled mixture of black, ecru, and white. The underparts are barred and vermiculated with black, rufous, buffy, and dirty white. There is a distinct white band on the throat. The particularly long tarsus is very noticeable.

My husband and I and George B. Reynard, who is associated with the laboratory of Living Sound at Cornell University, have made many recordings of the Least Pauraque's voice since 1972. The species responds readily to the recordings of its own voice and to whistled imitations of one of its various calls. Reynard has given the following analysis of its vocalizations:

"The first and most notable sound is the clear, continuous, rising trill. Then there is the three-styllable phrase, adequately described by Bond as *"Pau-ra-kay."* A modification of this is also heard and has been recorded. It is a four-syllable sequence that says *"Pau-ra-ra-kay."* The three-syllable form is the most common, which had led to the local name of "To-ree- co." The rapidly uttered disturbance sounds *"kaweck, weck, weck, weck, weck, weck"* are somewhat rhythmic, but with irregular numbers of *"wecks"* given in any particular series. There are other sounds, too, of low intensity with a distinct rising inflection. There are also scratchy, fricative sounds and something like the note of a ground dove."

We have observed or heard the Least Pauraque in pine forests, broadleaf forests, and mixed forests from sea level up to an altitude of 800 meters. However, it is more abundant in dry areas at lower altitudes.

There are reasons why *Siphonorhis brewsteri* should be rare. Because it nests on the ground and roosts on or near the ground, it is subject to predation by introduced rats *(Rattus norvegicus* and *R. rattus)* and the mongoose *(Herpestes auropunctatus).* However, man is the bird's worst enemy. In spite of the laws in the Dominican Republic that forbid the slashing and burning of any new area, these outdated agricultural methods are still used. Even though lumbering operations are officially prohibited, the bird's habitat is still threatened by widespread charcoal burning, for example.

In Haiti the conditions are much worse. In our 13 years of study in the Sierra de Baoruco at the border between the two countries, my husband I have watched the forests of the neighboring country diminish and the denuded hills become dry and bare. From a plane, one can tell where the Dominican Republic ends and where Haitian territory begins by the disappearance of the forest.

Given the many localities from which this species is hereby reported for the first time, it becomes evident that the Least Pauraque has either gone unnoticed for several decades or has greatly increased its range since the 1920s. There is also the possibility that the almost complete destruction of its habitat in Haiti has increased the population in the Dominican Republic as birds from Haiti have moved east to Dominican forests. On the other hand, it should be noted that none of the explorations by Beck, Abbott, Peters, Bond, or Wetmore ever reached most areas in which we have discovered this bird. In all likelihood, it was there all along.

I am indebted to Albert Schwartz, Kenneth C. Parkes, and Allen Keith for constructive criticism which served to improve this paper in various stages of development.

A Living Jewel

The Emerald Hummingbird

Order:	Apodiformes
Family:	Trochilidae
Scientific name:	*Chlorostilbon swainsonii*
English name:	Hispaniolan Emerald Hummingbird
Spanish name:	Zumbador

This middle-sized endemic hummingbird is often found feeding on the nectar of the red-orange fuchsia plants that can tolerate the cold of the higher mountains of Hispaniola. The nectar of the pink-flowered parasite of the pine tree, called "El Conde," is also one of its favorite foods. In fact, anything that is pink or red attracts this species: *Buzonuco, cadillo,* wild fuchsia—the list is long.

When the Emerald Hummer is at rest on a dry twig it is easy to spot it, but when it has a background of dark green it blends in well with the landscape and, unless it moves, one can easily overlook this bird.

One day when we were studying near the place called Siberia in the Constanza area, in the Cordillera Central, a young boy came to visit us. He showed us a nest of this species about 20 yards from our camp. It was located on an exposed root of a shrub, so deftly camouflaged that, although it was in plain sight, it appeared to be part of the dry root. It was made of spider webs and adorned with lichens.

There were two white eggs in the nest. Two days later the eggs hatched. What delicate, fragile, and helpless bits of flesh! They looked top-heavy, with their long, straight bills. I inadvertently touched the root on which the nest was placed and immediately those bills were dancing around, begging for food. What a sight it was to see the adult bird poke her beak down the throats of those young ones. It didn't take long for the mother to accept us as part of the environment. We were able to get a beautiful series of photographs as the *pichones* grew and developed.

One cloudy day we tried to take pictures but found it too dark. My husband cleaned away some of the overhanging bracken ferns and other debris to let in more light. We needed that day-by-day documentation. We managed to get some less than satisfactory pictures, but in the afternoon the sun came out. We hurried to the site and set up the tripod. The mother had rearranged the bracken until the nest was again hidden.

We were entertained royally watching the babies grow. During the whole process, the male never put in an appearance. It was a prime example of *machismo.*

The male of this species appears very dark in the field, but actually is green with a slight wash of greenish bronze on the back. There is a dark stick-pin effect on the breast. Other characteristics include the intermediate size, the straight beak, the pinkish lower mandible, and the forked tail. The female is a lighter green on the upperparts, becoming whitish at the tip of the tail. There is a white spot back of the eye; the underparts are dull, whitish gray. The lower mandible is not as red as that of the male.

The Hispaniolan Emerald Hummingbird is a resident of the higher mountains, but during the winter months it will descend to lower levels as food becomes scarce in the higher elevations.

He Flirts His Metallic Tail

The Antillean Mango Hummingbird

Order:	Apodiformes
Family:	Trochilidae
Scientific name:	*Anthracothorax dominicus*
English name:	Antillean Mango Hummingbird
Spanish name:	Zumbador Grande, Picaflor, Colibri

The Antillean Mango Hummingbird is the largest and most colorful of the hummers in Hispaniola. It is from 4½ to 5 inches long, and it is the only hummingbird on the island with a decidedly curved bill. It is widespread and common in all parts of its range, from below sea-level to the highest mountains.

In the field the male generally appears to be a very dark, velvety green. However, when the light is right the green has a golden sheen; the gorget is iridescent. The tail is brick-red, bordered with blue. The female is even more colorful. The green of its back is lighter; the underparts are grayish, washed with a little green on the sides. The tail is brick-red, bordered with purple and tipped with white. The immature male has a gray breast with a dark streak down the middle; sometimes it is mottled with dark, depending on the age of the bird.

Because the Antillean Hummingbird is very territorial it is easy to photograph, for it returns from time to time to a favorite perch. For the more sophisticated photographer, a cactus, a bromeliad, a hibiscus or even a wild canna will provide a chance to snap a shot in mid-air. With patience there is no end to the color combinations or positions that the photographer can obtain. The bird is rather tame and seems to be skittish only when the sun shines on the metal of the photographic equipment. Then, instead of going directly to the flower, it hovers over the shiny spot and thus interrupts the shot. But it tends to become accustomed to the intruder, because it will not be deterred from visiting the flowers regularly.

In the wet forests, the red busonuco furnishes nectar. In the cultivated areas the pink blossoms of the tobacco plants are preferred, and in the deserts and drier localities the nectar of the bright orange agave and the yellow cactus is taken. Red seems to be the bird's favorite color.

There always seem to be a large supply of insects around the white-fringed blossoms of the Rose Apple tree (Pomarosa). The big dark hummer can often be seen hawking insects near the Pomarosa groves along the banks of the rivers. While watching the birds in this environment I discovered that they help with the work of pollenization. We have taken specimens that were so laden with pollen, the head was completely yellow. Several times I thought I had found a new species.

What fun it is to see the female hummer sit and rest on an exposed dry twig of a tree after a feeding session. The long, narrow tongue flicks in and out as if she were giving it a cleaning but I often wonder what purpose this really serves.

Several times I have been fortunate enough to see this species in courtship. The most spectacular display was observed in the dry forest of the Sierra de Baoruco, between Puerto Escondido and Pueblo Viejo. I must have come upon a lek as described by Alexander F. Skutch in his book *The Life of the Hummingbird*. There were so many male hummers grouped and feeding on a hillside covered with blooming agave plants that it made me dizzy trying to track down one specific bird. They were constantly in motion. All the time I watched I did not hear any vocalizations. Maybe that was because their voices were extremely high-pitched and hard for humans to hear, or it could be that this species has not developed a song. In all our wanderings, I have not heard a peep or a squeak out of the Mango Hummer (I use a hearing aid) but my husband assures me that when there is a clash over territory, there is a lot of squeaking and squealing.

I had been watching the lek for a while when a female appeared. Did the male make the first move, or did she choose her partner? Before I could wink, a male started flying in her direction, and began to fly in a U-formation, swift and regular, up and down, up and down. So fast was the flight I could not see wing beats. Then, on one of the down flights, the female joined the male and they flew together, straight up into the air and away.

The female takes full responsibility after copulation for nest-building, incubation, and care of the young. The nest of the Antillean Mango, like the nest of other hummingbirds, is a work of art. Sometimes it is placed as high as 40 feet from the ground, in the middle of a bare limb of any sized tree. It is made of spider-webs and decorated on the outside with lichens so arranged that the nest looks like a knot on the branch, a perfect camouflage.

Once when I was collecting material for a diorama for the Museum of Natural History I found an abandoned nest of the Antillean Mango Hummingbird. I carefully removed it and took notes on its location, size, and construction materials. When I opened the plastic bag containing it, in the lab, I found a hundred million (more or less) little mites crawling everywhere. We took some specimens for the lab technician and then I sprayed it all with an insecticide. The nest disintegrated, leaving only the lichens. Spider webs make a soft material that looks like spun silk, but the webs do not stand up under the solvent in the spray. Or could the disappearance of all the mites have caused the nest to collapse?

Two white eggs are laid. I have never had the opportunity to monitor an incubating Mango Hummingbird's nest so I cannot say how long it takes for the babies to hatch. But I do know that the little birds that emerge are almost naked except for a little fuzz on the back. Their eyes are bulged and shut, and the beak is only a nubbin. Ugly little things, but they do turn into beautiful creatures later on.

This species seems to be particularly prolific. We have seen an Antillean Mango building a new nest even while she is still feeding an older brood. It appears that there is no specific time for procreation. We have found nests in nearly every month of the year, with the exception of December and January.

My husband has done extensive photography of each of the Hispaniolan hummingbirds. Here is a firsthand report of an experience he had with our Mango:

"In the xerophytic northwestern part of the Dominican Republic I was instrumental in bringing about the creation of a sanctuary to protect the only remaining area known to harbor the very rare Bee Orchid, *Oncidium henekenii*. The President of the Republic by decree set aside some 200 tareas (33 acres) which were assigned to the National Parks to administer and to the Botanical Gardens (my employer) to direct.

"Before a protecting fence had been erected, I spent many hours a day studying the pollinator of the orchid, which resembles a very small bumblebee. While I sat observing the orchid, I became aware of the many hummingbirds, both the Mango and the Vervain, that visited the colorful blossoms of the cacti, legumes and even bromeliads. In fact, when I was questioned by the local people about my activities, I always told them I was studying the birds. And I was.

"One day, near the edge of the sanctuary where I was camped, I saw a female 'Mango' whiz around one of our big 'paddle cacti' *Consolea moniliformis*. "This particular plant, at about ten feet in height, was short compared with some of the 15-footers. I went around behind the cactus just in time to see the mother perch on the edge of the nest to feed her little baby. Its mouth was agape and she hunched up and over to poke her long beak into its mouth. Then, with a rapid up-and-down motion like a sewing-machine needle, she 'pumped' her goodies into its throat.

"In a few seconds she flew away and began her unceasing round of the cactus flowers and of the small trumpet-shaped blossom of *Distactis latiflora* growing on a sparsely leaved vine that frequently climbs over the cacti. In ten or fifteen minutes she returned but her pumping session was short. As the sun rose higher, the mother's visits became less frequent and the little one showed signs of heat prostration. The nest was perched on the edge of one of the paddles (not leaves) and resembled a cactus apple that grew in the same position not far away. The little fellow stretched its head over the edge of the nest and let it hang down. Perhaps he hoped to find shade on that side.

"After observing this ludicrous but pitiful sight, I began to think of ways to help. I dug up an old medicine dropper and filled it with sugared water. Since I was taking pictures of the feeding process with my camera and tripod on top of my Volkswagen bus, I had a ladder available. I carefully placed it against the cactus trunk, climbed up, and stretched out to the nest.

"The mother, aroused by my intrusion, buzzed anxiously about me and finally settled down almost 20 feet away. Touching the tip of the dropper to the tip of the baby's beak, I squeezed a little syrup out. Nothing happened. I did it again, but there was no interest. Finally I wedged the eye-dropper between two paddles and climbed down. Hardly had I walked over to the shade of the car when the mother whizzed over to the little tube. After examining it with her beak, she placed the tip of her bill at the mouth of the dropper, ran her tongue up in it, and in a flash drained it. Just as quickly she flew over to the little one and carefully gave him another fast food session.

"Then she flew back to the eye-dropper, but it held no more. So off to the watching perch she flew. I, of course, happy at the success of my feeding, refilled and replaced the dropper and returned to the shade. Again she came to the sweet tooth and, with no hesitation this time, drained it.

"Instead of going directly to the nest she flew up to the perch and evidently swallowed the nectar for herself. After another refill she fed the baby again, finally flying away. She did not return for some time; perhaps she was hunting insects to provide a little protein in the diet.

"I decided to try to feed the young bird again, and when I dribbled a little of the sweetness on its beak it opened wide and I gave it a few drops. It opened up again and I let it have a bit more. Finally my wife called to warn me of over-feeding and with that reminder I climbed down.

"In a short time the female returned to the nest and fed the chick but did not go to the perch. Instead she flew to the car window and, placing her beak on the glass, cruised up and down, watching herself in the reflection all the while. I stood fascinated at how she was accepting all of my interventions with the car and camera, and finally the nectar and the ladder. As if in answer to my wondering, she zapped over to me and put her beak to my glasses and gave me a buzzing-over. I stood very still, for it was my first experience with being 'kissed' by a hummer.

"My wife and I talked over my experiences with the 'injection' feeding and decided that the birds would have to make it on their own. However, I decided to rig up a shade for the nest. I found an old board and wedged it over the nest to protect it from the overhead sun.

"The next morning we visited other places near the sanctuary, but before we left we drove down to see how the improvised parasol was working. When I got there, the little one was sitting up all pert and cheery. I hope I may be pardoned because of my imagining that it directed a look of thanks at me as I left."

Thus endeth the saga of the love affair that my husband had with the beautiful Mango Hummingbird. He has some extraordinarily striking photographs and a wealth of pleasant memories in payment for his patience and work.

A Mighty Mite

The Vervain Hummingbird

Order:	Apodiformes
Family:	Trochilidae
Scientific name:	*Mellisuga minima*
English name:	Vervain Hummingbird
Spanish name:	Zumbadorcito

Look sharply! What you think is a bee or an insect may turn out to be the Vervain Hummingbird! It measures only six centimeters and weighs 1.6 grams, but, for its size, it is one of our most vociferous and aggressive birds. Many are the times I have seen Red-tailed hawks, Gray Kingbirds, and Kestrels flee its sharp beak. Its song, although high-pitched, can be heard often and for some distance. You can generally locate the bird by listening for its vocalizations.

The Vervain Hummingbird often appears black and white in the field, according to the amount of light that reaches its plumage. When the bird is perched on a dry twig of a tree on a bright sunny day, you can see that it is green on the upper parts and white on its lower parts. The throat is speckled with gold-colored spots and sometimes you can see gold iridescence on the back. The primary wing feathers are dark purple. The female lacks the speckled throat and has some white on the margin of the tail.

The tiny bird prefers the nectar and pollen from bright red flowers but will also visit white, yellow, and blue ones. Since it is difficult for such a small creature to reach deep into a large flower, the minute bird will often make a hole in the side to reach the center. Small insects from the flower are included in the diet of nectar and pollen. At times we have even observed the little fellow hawking insects from a perch.

One season we had the incredible luck to find a Vervain Hummingbird's nest close to my husband's office in the Botanical Garden. The tiny white eggs were laid in a nest no bigger than a large thimble. The cup was formed mostly of spider web and was beautifully adorned with lichens. It was located in a mango tree on a low branch, about 3½ to 4 feet from the ground.

The day after finding the nest my husband went to the site to take pictures and found there was only one egg. Upon doing some heavy detective work, he learned that a young employee of the garden had snitched one egg to see if he could incubate it at home. The next day the whole nest, with the second egg, was gone. This time we were really indignant. We found out that another worker had taken the entire nest to use as a cure for an earache!

Luckily for us, the little hummingbird was undaunted. Another nest was promptly made on the same twig and after several lectures and threats from my husband the workers left the little mother alone. We were able to document the whole process by movie camera and everyone was happy when the two young ones left the nest.

The female does all the work of procreation: nest-building, incubation, and care of the young. The male never even comes near the nest. For that reason many Dominicans call all hummingbirds "Don Juan." When I asked why, I was answered, "Pican la flor y se van!" Translated, that means, "They take the best of the flower and go!"

A Barking Dog with Geranium-red Underparts

The Hispaniolan Trogon

Order:	Trogoniformes
Family:	Trogonidae
Scientific name:	*Temnotrogon roseigaster*
English name:	Hispaniolan Trogon
Spanish name:	Papagayo, Cotorrita de Sierra, Loro, Piragua

The Trogons are birds of the tropics. In the West Indies they live only on the islands of Cuba and Hispaniola, each island having its own endemic species.

A Barking Dog with Geranium-red Underparts

The Hispaniolan Trogon is one of our most beautiful birds. It is about the size of a large pigeon; it has a small head, a short, orange-colored bill, a long tail, and brilliant plumage. The head and the upper parts are a lustrous green, the throat is dark gray, the breast is pale gray, and the abdomen "geranium" red. The tail is laddered with white and turquoise blue. The wings of the male are finely checkered with black and white, while the female's are plain black. The eye is bright yellow-orange. In the breeding season it becomes a conspicuous bright red.

The Trogon has a characteristic pose that helps to identify it in the field. When at rest the head is drawn upon the shoulders; the feet are covered by the abdominal feathers and the tail hangs straight down. The bird is quite tame and at times it seems very lethargic.

For the most part the Trogons travel in pairs, keeping contact with each other by their calls. It is hard for a bird-watcher to locate them, however, because the quality of the voice makes it sound as if a ventriloquist is at work. The song can be heard all through the forest: "Coc-carr-rao, Coc-carr-rao." There are several interesting variations. Most noticeable are the staccato notes of disturbance. They are reminiscent of a puppy barking and after several renditions the bird is easily located.

The pair does not feed together but they search together for tree cavities for nesting. They work together to make it a home, then two beautiful pale green eggs are laid. Their diet consists mainly of wild fruits and insects; the fruit from the parrot tree seems to be the bird's favorite food. It is a beautiful, never-to-be-forgotten privilege to see a Trogon hawk for insects. The flight and the display of colors are incredible.

Once when we were in the mountains in the Baoruco Range, near Loma de Toro, an ornithologist in our group wanted to take a female Trogon for the scientific collection at the Museum of Natural History, where he was working. Since he already had a male, he wanted to complete the pair.

Early one morning he was successful in obtaining a female a short distance from camp. All day long the Trogons sang around us, but one song stood out as very different. It was sad, urgent, and anxious. Thinking that the call might be that of an unknown species, the collector followed the sounds until he came upon a male Trogon sitting in the same tree where its mate had been taken. It was still there the next day, singing its plaintive call, but finally toward evening it flew away.

The Hispaniolan Trogon is listed as "locally common" in the 1931 Bulletin #155 from the Smithsonian Institution and it is still quite common in the higher mountains where there are still virgin forests. In some of the private plantations of the Cordillera Septentrional the birds can be seen occasionally in the hilly country, on abandoned coffee farms or in old cacao groves. In the Cordillera Central the recent destruction along the highways has caused a drastic decrease in the Trogon population in that area. In the Sierra de Baoruco, where there has been much less people-impact, the melodious calls still ring out over the mountainsides and the birds themselves can be seen flashing their colors in the early morning sun.

However, during the winter months when it gets very cold in the mountains and food becomes scarce, the Trogons descend to lower elevations.I have seen them regularly at 500 meters in woodlands (mostly pines) near the Hotel Montaña on the road to Jarabacoa. From November through February I have seen them on the flat between Puerto Escondido and Aguacate in the Baoruco Range. Once we saw a pair in the desert forest on the crest of the hill between Las Cruces de Puerto Escondido and Lago Enriquillo.

The Hispaniola Trogon has been known on this island since the time of Buffon (1779) and although it is recognized as beautiful and beneficial, it is very vulnerable because like the parakeet and the parrot it is taken for food in some localities.

The Deceptive Little Green Todies

The Broad-billed Tody

Order:	Coraciiformes
Family:	Todidae
Scientific name:	*Todus subulatus* and
	Todus angustirostris
English name:	Broad-billed Tody and
	Narrow-billed Tody
Spanish name:	Barrancoli, and the Chicuí

At first glance, a tody could be confused with a hummingbird because of its small size, brilliant colors, and longish bill. At second glance, one might think it belonged to the flycatcher family because of its habit of catching insects on the wing. But actually it

The Narrow-billed Tody

is not even related to either of these families; its closest relative is the kingfisher.

For many years the ornithologists believed that there was only once species of tody on the island of Hispaniola and that the differences between the specimen that came from the high mountains and the ones from the lowlands were sexual and geographical. Now we know that there are two species: *Todus subulatus*, which lives at elevations up to 3,000 feet, and *Todus angustirostris*, which lives at higher altitudes. In the unique environment of the Haitises (Cockpit Country), however, both species live side by side but do not interbreed. It seems that *T. angustirostris* is the more adaptable species, because it does live at lower levels whereas *T. subulatus* is never found in the higher altitudes.

The todies are truly jewels in the world of birds, especially during the breeding season when every color is intensified. The green coloration gives them a natural camouflage but the bright red throat spot is easily discerned.

T. subulatus, the Broad-billed Tody, is about 4½ inches long. Its green upperparts are washed with a yellowish gold cast. The underparts are grayish, tinged with pink on the sides and pale yellow on the lower abdomen. It has a large, bright red throat patch. The beak is wide at the base and is completely bright red. Its call is distinctive: *"Terp, terp, terp,"* all on the same note.

T. angustirostris, the Narrow-billed Tody, is slightly smaller; it measures 4¼ inches in length. It is brilliant dark green on the upper parts, and a grayish white on the underparts. The sides are washed with pink; the lower underparts are very slightly tinged with pale yellow. The throat patch is bright red. The beak is long and slender with a black tip. The call of the Narrow-billed Tody is a distinctive two-syllable call that sounds like *"Chi-cuí, chi-cuí,"* from whence comes the Dominican common name Chicuí. Both species make a very peculiar rattle-like sound, which was thought to be caused by wing movement, but we have found that this is a type of vocalization.

The young of both species lack the bright-red throat patch. The upper parts are dull green; the lower parts are gray; and the throat is streaked with black. As the bird assumes adult plumage, the throat becomes red with white spots which eventually disappear. Both species have been found with green eyes as well as brown eyes. The reason for this is unknown, since the phenomenon occurs in the immature as well as in adults and in both sexes.

Both species nest in tunnels that the pair excavates in banks of any kind. I have seen tody holes in the deep ruts of a little-used road, in banks along the side of the road, and in river banks. The two take turns working. One sits on a dry twig or a branch of a low tree while the partner digs. In about three minutes you will see the dirt falling out of a hole in the bank and a tiny green bird appears. It exchanges places with the bird perched on the twig and there it sits until the dirt again comes flying out of the hole. This continues until a tunnel about 12 inches long is made. The tunnel is never straight; it is curved at the end to hide the nest from sight. Two to five white eggs are laid on the ground, in a slight depression at the end of the diggings.

A word of warning to inquisitive people. Do not put your hand in tody holes. Sometimes other creatures have taken up residence in nests that have been abandoned. You may be surprised to find a large, hairy spider or a snake (non-poisonous) or some kind of stinging insect.

In my work I have often had to use mist nets, and since the todies are very common, I have always caught at least a half dozen in every trip to the field. Their small size and rather weak flight make it easy for them to fall into the loops of the net and become entangled on both sides. After a short struggle, the birds seem to give up and become limp, making it a real chore to remove them. In fact the birds appear to be dead.

How many times have I laid a "dead" bird on the ground, only to have it revive immediately and fly away! Do they really play dead? Or do they know that struggling only makes them more entangled? One day a tody was found caught in a spider web. It appeared to be dead, but when my husband opened his hand to show the bird to me it flew away so fast that all you could see was a little green streak.

Todus subulatus can be seen on the grounds of the Zoological Park and in the Gran Cañada in the Botanical Garden in Santo Domingo or in low elevations anywhere, wherever there is an appropriate nesting place. *Todus angustirostris*, the high-mountain species, may be found in La Colonia, back of Cambita Carabitos, not far from the capital. Both species are found in Los Haitises and in the Parque del Este.

The todies live only in the Greater Antilles, that is, Cuba, Jamaica, Puerto Rico, and Hispaniola. Each island has its own endemic species; only Hispaniola has two.

The Little Bird with the Big Voice

The Hispaniolan Piculet

Order:	Piciformes
Family:	Picidae,
	Sub-family Picumninae
Scientific name:	*Nesoctites micromega*
English name:	Hispaniolan Piculet
Spanish name:	Carpintero Bolo,
	Carpinterito de Sierra,
	Tu-tu-lo-feo, Flautero,
	Gur-ru-pió

The piculet is known throughout the Dominican Republic as the little bird with the big voice. Even though its call is often heard and is known in every environment, the piculet is not frequently seen. The protective coloration of its plumage and the ventriloquist quality of its voice, together with its habit of sitting perfectly still for long periods, make it almost impossible to locate. We have made many safaris into the interior of the island, looking for the piculet. We recorded the song long before we could spy the bird. It was when we used the recording as bait during the courting session that we finally succeeded in getting a good look at the little fellow. Even though it took us four years, we feel it was time well spent.

We saw some beautiful new country and had some happy but also some very frustrating experiences. We did make many new friends, learned a great deal about *campesino* folklore and superstitions, and found out many new regional names for our elusive, fugitive piculet. In the Cordillera Central it is called the "Gur-rupió" by some; others call it the "Carpinterito de Sierra" (Little Woodpecker of the Mountains). In the Sierra de Baoruco it is known as "Tu-tu-lo-feo" and in the east where it is most common in the humid forests it is called the Carpintero Bolo. In still other places it is named the "Flautero" (flutist).

Our first long safari took us to the mountains of the Sierra de Ocoa in the central range, in February, 1974. We were accompanied by Dr. George B. Reynard. We had left our car in the mountain village of Valdesia and hiked three hours to an abandoned *bohío* (hut) on an old coffee plantation. We had a mule to carry our overnight equipment and the recording apparatus. The trail was steep and dry, narrow and rocky, making progress very slow. We also had to be on the alert because the beast that carried the equipment was flighty and balky, which made the going even more hazardous. It was dark before we made camp.

My husband, Dr. Reynard, and the guide were very solicitous about my welfare. They decided that I should sleep in the *bohío*, where there was a built-in cot. I will admit I was glad to get the cot. I have an innate fear of the big, black centipedes that live in the damp leaf mould of the humid forests and sleeping on the ground makes me uneasy. However, the night I had the cot I slept with creatures other than centipedes.

The *campesinos* who lived there during the coffee harvest had left some chickens that used the house as a roost. As a result I woke up the next morning to find myself literally covered with crawling mites. I had been too tired to notice them during the night. We worked long and hard for two days but saw nary a piculet. The next week, while at work in the health center in the village, a piculet sang at the top of its lungs from a leafy *limoncillo* tree right outside my office window!

We were finally able to see the piculet up close when we caught a pair in a dry forest outside Villa Eliza, in the northwest. We had heard them conversing but were surprised to find that they flew close enough to the ground to be caught in a mist net. We had a hard time getting them untangled because they are pugnacious, active, and most vociferous. We got some very good pictures and were able to describe the birds at close range.

The upper parts of the Hispaniolan Piculet are greenish-brown with the hind neck spotted with white. The underparts are whitish or yellowish-white streaked with black. The sexes are similar, except for the bright yellow crown. The male has this spot centered with bright red.

The form of the bird as well as its behavior help in the identification. Its small size (5½ to 6 inches) along with the short, soft tail gives it the round appearance from whence comes one of the local names, the Carpintero Bolo—in English, the Little Round Woodpecker. It creeps along the branches of trees, looking for insects that live on the bark. It does not drill holes when looking for food. It does not use the tail as a brace while climbing, giving the impression of a nuthatch or sparrow.

When the pair becomes separated, they make contact with each other by calling. One day I discovered a female perched in a dead tree, in plain sight. I moved carefully behind a baitoa tree where there was some shade, since it was already hot at 9 a.m. and I knew I would be waiting for a while. I had no way of knowing how long the bird had been sitting there before I discovered it but about three minutes after I was settled with my binoculars focused, the bird sang. I did not hear an answer and evidently the bird didn't either because it sat perfectly still. Five minutes later it called again, and again there was no answer. About 9:15 the bird sang again, and this time an answer came from across a clearing. The perched bird immediately took off toward the edge of the forest in the direction from which the sound had come.

During the courtship period we have seen and heard drumming; the male is particularly pugnacious in the defense of its territory and there are many physical encounters. The pair makes the nest in holes in the trees, posts, or cactus, where they take turns excavating a relatively small hole.

To see a piculet one must have patience, persistence, and a great measure of luck. A good pair of eyes, a good pair of binoculars, and someone to tell you where there is a good population would also be helpful. But don't expect to see the Hispaniolan Piculet on your first visit into the countryside. Then, if you do happen to be lucky enough, you can be pleasantly surprised!

Friend or Foe?

The Hispaniolan Woodpecker

Order:	Piciformes
Family:	Picidae
Scientific name:	*Melanerpes striatus*
English name:	Hispaniolan Woodpecker
Spanish name:	Carpintero

Our abundant, beautiful, and endemic Hispaniolan Woodpecker has been the cause of controversy and discussion for almost 500 years, ever since agricultural pursuits were begun on the island. Because of its peculiar behavior and its extraordinary structural form, its scientific classification has been changed at least seven times.

Even though the Department of Agriculture has declared it a destructive enemy to certain crops, and has paid bounties on its tongue (as proof of death) for decades, the bird is still abundant; in fact it is one of our most common birds.

The secret of its survival is its capacity to adapt to any and all of our various environments. This species lives everywhere from below sea-level around Lake Enriquillo to the highest point in all the Antilles, Pico Duarte. The bird's strident voice fills every corner of every kind of habitat, be it desert, piney woods, broadleaf forests or mangroves. The diet is so varied that it always has a food supply. Food, juices, insects of many kinds, and berries are all on the diet list, but I have noticed that it has a particular fondness for the ripe fruit of the almacigo tree. These small berries are given as first food to the woodpecker nestlings. Fruit from the Royal Palm is also taken, and the trunk of this common tree is often home base for several families.

However, when there are no palms, any other kind of tree will do if it is the right size. In one place in the Northwest, where the trees are small, Hispaniolan Woodpeckers were found nesting in banks along the road. Some naturalists on the island think that the presence of a large number of wasps may have influenced the birds to seek refuge in the earth, but I do not agree. The wasps are not known to bother birds; in fact, the Village Weaver seeks out places where wasps are found and presumably uses them as protection from predators. This seemingly aberrant action on the part of the woodpecker shows how adaptable it can be and how capable it is of coping with unfavorable situations.

Even if the woodpecker is aggressive and rude, and threatens with its loud voice, a group of them once yielded to some seemingly peaceful Purple Martins *(Progne dominicensis)*. One year we found an old, dried-up palm tree in the Botanical Gardens where five or six pairs of woodpeckers had made their nests. The next year, the nests were taken over by the Purple Martins. I thought the nests had been abandoned by their former owners, but when I talked to the guard who observed them daily it was a different story. The swallows had driven the woodpeckers away and had taken the holes for their own. "It was a real battle, Doña," the man said. "They fought for several days before the woodpeckers stayed away!"

The Hispaniolan Woodpecker has developed certain characteristics that contribute to its survival. The nests are placed high in the trees where they experience minimal molestation. There are seldom less than four eggs in a clutch, which leads one to believe that nesting success is common and there is a low mortality rate. Several books on woodpeckers describe the males as industrious and doing the lion's share of the work of rearing the young. The Hispaniolan woodpecker certainly does not live up to that reputation so far as feeding is concerned. In January, 1983, I observed a family of woodpeckers in the Botanical Garden for several days. The female made four or five trips to the nest to each one made by the male. Often he would be perched nearby, eating almacigo fruit or preening while the female carried the berries to the nest and regurgitated them one by one until the nestlings were fed. She was the one that cleaned the nest and carried away the excreta and chitins. Maybe that particular female had not yet heard of women's liberation.

Our woodpecker is the victim of at least three different kinds of internal parasites and often has lice and warble fly infestations. However, these do not seem to diminish the population.

So what difference does it make to *Melanerpes striatus* if there is controversy, persecution, and problems of scientific identification? It seems to be happy to be flying its undulating flight and calling out in its raucous voice, *"Killi, killi, killi."*

We conservationists do not worry about its present condition. It seems to be equipped to survive.

An Overlooked Flycatcher

The Greater Antillean Elaenia

Order:	Passeriformes
Family:	Tyrannidae
Scientific name:	*Elaenia fallax*
English name:	Greater Antillean Elaenia
Spanish name:	Maroita canosa

In spite of having driven long and hard the day before, we woke up early that morning. It was cold and dark; we couldn't see much beauty at 5 a.m. It was difficult to make ourselves crawl out of our sleeping bags, but we were ravenous. The fresh mountain air and the long night had given us a good appetite, and we wanted to be ready to work at the crack of dawn.

An Overlooked Flycatcher

We were on a expedition to Loma de Toro, in the Sierra de Baorucco, close to the frontier between the Dominican Republic and the Republic of Haiti. We were recording bird songs and collecting specimens for the National Museum of Natural History, as well as searching for orchids for the herbarium of the National Botanical Garden. By daybreak we had eaten our breakfast and had cleaned up the camp. Armed with binoculars, field guide, camera, tools for orchid collecting, rain gear, and our lunch, we locked up the van and started out.

We hadn't gone far when all of a sudden the pine forest around us burst into a chorus of bird songs. We could distinguish various vocalizations: the Chat tanager, the La Selle's Thrush, the Pine Warbler, the Solitaire. A Narrow-billed Tody repeated his *"Chi-cuí"* over and over again, while a Trogon kept calling out, *"Coc-coc-carr-arao!"* Then, right over our heads, we heard a sprightly trill that we did not recognize.

It didn't take us long to locate the author of the song. At first it was hard to see anything of color in the early, gray light of the morning, but we could see the silhouette. It had a smallish head, slender body, and a longish tail. And we could distinguish the white wing bars. That was enough to identify the songster as the *Elaenia fallax*. Conditions were favorable, and for the the first time in history the dawn song was recorded.

The *Elaenia fallax* was first reported from the Dominican Republic by the French naturalist, Vieillot, in 1807. It was described as new to science and given the name of *Muscicapa albicapilla*. There was nothing written about its habits, its form, or its family. After that, there was no mention made of the bird until 1847 when it was listed by Hartlaub as *Tyrannus albicapilla*. In 1895 it was "rediscovered" by Cherrie and described by Cory, who evidently did not know of its previous history. He announced it as new to science, using the name of *Elaenia cherri* in honor of the person who had supposedly discovered the bird.

Other ornithologists collected specimens, but still nothing new was noted about the bird's life history. Verrill, Abbott, Wetmore,

Ciferri, and Hartert all commented on its being common in the higher elevations and remarked on its sprightly song. But finally, some time after 1931, it was studied scientifically and given the name of *Elaenia fallax*.

The Greater Antillean Elaenia was still relatively unknown to the Dominicans when we made our first long camping trip to the Loma de Toro in 1972. We brought back specimens, recordings of its song, and scientific facts about its life history. After reporting these findings to Dr. Eugenio de Jesús Marcano, the leading Dominican naturalist at the time, he gave it its first common Dominican name, Maroita Canosa, because of the white spot on the crown.

The Maorita Canosa is about 15 centimeters long. It is quite slender, and appears more so because of its longish tail. It has a small beak for a flycatcher, not as wide or as flat as would be expected. It is quite ordinary in color, being olive-gray on the upper parts, but in the springtime it can be seen to have a greenish cast. The wings are darker and have two wing bars of dirty white. The under parts are a beautiful, light yellow. There is a white patch on the crown that is not easily seen in the field.

The nest of the *Elaenia fallax* is generally located in a shrub or a low tree and is a cup made of moss, lined with feathers. The eggs are quite distinctly spotted, but the spots are few and far between.

The bird's diet includes small fruits and berries that happen to be in season as well as insects that are captured on the wing.

Once when we were in the Cordillera Central between Siberia and La Nevera (The Ice Box) we put up our mist nets and what a harvest of Elaenias we had! They were so active and aggressive that we had a hard time getting them out of the nets, until finally we had to "close down." These birds had been eating blackberries or some other purple-colored fruit. The net was literally covered with a sticky purple excreta by the time we had gotten the last captive free.

The Commander of the Army Post in nearby Constanza chose that particular time to pay a visit to our camp. He wanted to present his wife and three children to some real naturalists. How could I shake hands with our new friends at that moment? I excused myself and tried to explain why I was keeping my hands in my pockets. "¡Está Ud. en su oficio, Señora! ¡Está en su oficio!" (You are doing your job!), he exclaimed. But they didn't stay long. He must have guessed that it wasn't exactly the psychological moment to impress the young people with the joys of being a naturalist.

The Greater Antillean Elaenia is still relatively unknown in the Dominican Republic. Due to its restricted range of the high mountain habitat, its unobtrusive habits, and its drab coloration, it is very easily overlooked. Because of the lack of water and the very cold weather, few people live in the hostile environment that the bird now occupies. Only the most motivated and dedicated naturalists venture into its territory. No wonder it is still overlooked by most Dominicans.

In all likelihood the *Elaenia fallax* was found at lower elevations when first discovered by Vieillot in 1807. Since that time the lowland pine forests have been completely destroyed, and the bird has been driven higher and higher in order to live in its preferred niche. The lowest elevation in which we have ever encountered it is about 1,000 meters, near Loma de Yautia, not far from Rancho Arriba.

The Greater Antillean Elaenia is endemic to Jamaica and Hispaniola.

When Green Turns to Gold

The Golden Swallow

Order:	Passeriformes
Family:	Hirundinidae
Scientific name:	Kalochelidon euchrysea
English name:	Golden Swallow
Spanish name:	Golondrina verde
	(Green Swallow)

A group of young people from the Ornithological Society of Santo Domingo asked my husband and me to be their leaders for their monthly excursion. They were anxious to hear and see some of the mountain birds about which I had written in my Nature column in the Saturday Supplement of the newspaper, *El Caribe.*

We started early one morning in May, 1975 as it was the beginning of the season when many species start a new nesting cycle. We hoped we would have a fine day, but we also remembered that it was the beginning of the rainy season.

We arrived at the summit of the watershed about 7:30 a.m. It was cold and damp with patchy fog, but the sun was peeking through the mist every now and then. We stopped for breakfast coffee just before we reached the settlement on the road to Rancho Arriba. About 15 minutes later we began to look for birds. At about 8 o'clock the whole area seemed to come awake with the sound of bird songs. We heard a pair of piculets answering each other, some narrow-billed todies were chirruping, a black-whiskered vireo began to repeat a welcome, *"Bien-te-veo, bien-te-veo."* We saw a Red-tailed Hawk, a Sharp-shinned Hawk and a flock of Palm Crows came to see what we were doing. A Lizard Cuckoo sounded off, and the brightly colored Stripe-headed Tanager flew by. Everyone of our group had an opportunity to see each bird clearly. What a thrill! Most of the group had never visited the high mountains (3300ft. elevation) before, and each bird was entirely new.

Slowly we worked our way down to the northeast side of a deep ravine. When we looked below us we could see a trail that wound around the contour of the mountain, always going deeper and deeper into the ravine. There, on a sort of a natural look-out we could observe two Red-tailed Hawks circling and how a tiny humming bird was harassing first one then the other. A Sharp shinned Hawk crashed through some low branches not far from us as it chased an unwary warbler, and a Cuckoo called again. Someone said, "I see a Buteo, but it doesn't have a red tail." And sure enough! We saw a pair of Ridgway's Hawks hunting. Even at that time these endemic hawks were seldom seen in the Cordillera Central. And about the same time someone spotted the Golden Swallows. The air over the ravine seemed to be full of them, darting, sailing, gliding, turning, always moving and vocalizing softly. *"Chee-weet, chee-wet."* There were so many birds we could actually hear their voices.

"These birds must nest in colonies," I said. "Let's read what the book tells us about them."

"But the book is written in English. You read it to us, Profesora."

I read from the Field Guide to the Birds of the West Indies. Translating to Spanish, I read, "A beautiful swallow that somewhat resembles the Tree Swallow but is smaller and more delicate and graceful in appearance, with relatively longer wings and a more deeply forked tail. The upper parts are emerald green, glossed with bluish and strongly with gold; underparts are white. The inmature are duller above and have a gray band across the breast."

"Why is it called a Golden Swallow when it is green?" questioned another member of the group.

"Because in the sun the feathers are tinged with gold, and are irridescent, the way the hummingbird's feathers are. But I think our name in Spanish has a better sound."

"Does it say anything about the habits of the bird?"

"Why don't you write a book for us in Spanish, Doña Tudy?" It was at that monent when I decided that a book in Spanish on the Dominican Birds was a necessity and that I would write it!

There is nothing about life histories in Bond's book, but it did say that the bird is found chiefly in high elevations, in cloud forests as well as in more open country.

That day we discovered that the Golden Swallows *did* nest in colonies, in cavities in dead trees, mostly on horizontal branches. We stood on our natural platform for perhaps 15 minutes. The sun came out and shone so brightly that every drop of water glistened with reflections like a thousand mini-suns. But the sun was too bright to last long. We all knew it could cloud over quickly and there could be a torrential downpour in a matter of minutes, but it wasn't likely so early in the morning. Soon we noticed that the swallows were going in and out of a thicket of Yagrumo trees *(Cecropia peltata)*. We decided to go down the steep trail to investigate.

The going was easy downhill, even if the trail was as slippery as a greased pig. We made hand holds of the vegetation and slid most of the way. We arrived at the thicket in jig time and, trying not to disturb the birds. we spread out and sat down to watch the ever active flock.

The birds paid no attention to us. They flitted and darted in and out and finally a single bird with no hesitation flew directly into a hole in a horizontal dead limb of a Yagrumo tree. Soon another bird came and clung to the side of the hole, making an urgent sound. Shortly after that there was a muffled chirp and out came the first swallow, the waiting one slipping in immediately. Then the first one returned with insects in its mouth, and the exchange of birds was made. This process was repeated for several times until finally both birds stayed away from the hole for a time. After that we found more than a dozen nests in about four or five trees.

We never saw the nestlings because the trees were situated too high for us to see inside, but we do know that there must have been several nestlings in each hole inasmuch as the parent birds were making such frequent trips to the nests.

We found several other birds that made the morning memorable. We heard the *"Chip, chip, chip-chip-chip"* of the Chat Tanagers, but we saw not a one. We saw the tiny hummingbird again hassling the hawks, We saw a hawk's nest on the stub of a tall pine tree. We even saw spit bugs, the first I had ever seen in the tropics. It was exciting to tell the students about their pecularities. We found some Narrow Billed Tody nests along the banks of the trail, and marvelled that they were so close to the level of the trail. The birds make their nests in tunnels and sometimes other animals usurp the nests. I warned the group about putting their hands in the Tody holes. It is not pleasant to encounter a centipede or a tarantula that has set up housekeeping inside.

We lost all track of time until we heard a loud roll of thunder. There is nothing more terrifying than being caught in a tropical storm. With one accord we all turned our faces to the upward trail. With the second clap of thunder the rain started. We cut some banana leaves for each person to use as an umbrella, but in that downpour they were riddled shortly. We had quite a ways to climb. The ground was already wet and the vegetation pulled out easily if we tried to haul ourselves along by grabbing it. We fell frequently. We were soon soaking wet.

Naked wet clay is not easy to walk on. We finally tried to walk on all fours. That was such slow work that by the time we reached the place where we had stepped across a tiny stream going down, we found a raging torrent. Every time a bolt of lightning came we shivered. We were vulnerable and we knew it. We found a place away from the water and huddled together for warmth and comfort. We had to wait for almost 45 minutes before we could cross the stream and make our way to the top.

We sought shelter at the first hut we saw, and we almost filled the room. The lady of the house gave us some home roasted coffee to warm us up and immediately warned us to dry our heads and change into dry clothing before we caught a bad cold. Our bird watching for that day, however, was not over. When the rain stopped and we had eaten our lunch we all felt better. We stayed close to the highway and continued to enjoy the bird life of the high mountains again. We saw Trogons, an Elaenia, woodpeckers by the dozens. The Solitaire tantalized us by singing from concealed perches, but we did not see a single one. We stayed on, hoping to see some nightjars or an owl or two, but our luck had run out, as far as birding was concerned. However, we were happy and everyone considered that we were lucky to be alive!

Several days after our trip to Rancho Arriba we saw an article in the *El Caribe* that two young boys had been struck by lightning in the area where we had been bird watching. One had died, the other in serious condition. They had sought shelter from the storm under some palm trees.

The Golden Swallow is endemic to Jamaica and to the Island of Hispaniola. When we first started our bird studies in 1968, this species was common in the mountain areas of the Cordillera Central and of the Sierra de Baoruco, but rare in a few places of the Cordillera Septentrional. Since the swallows' food consists solely of insects captured on the wing, there is always a good supply of food. But the depletion of the forests has destroyed their nesting sites, diminishing reproduction, and numbers have declined in all parts of its range.

A Crow is a Crow in Any Language

The White-necked Crow

Order: Passeriformes
Family: Corvidae
Scientific name: *Corvus leucognaphalus*
English name: White-necked Crow
Spanish name: El Cuervo

There are two representatives of the crow family on the Island of Hispaniola, the White-necked Crow and the Palm Crow. Like all other members of the family, they have a bad reputation. They are called thieves and gluttons, rude, noisy, gross, and belligerent. Perhaps it is because of these same characteristics that they have been able to adapt to civilization and survive better than any of the other birds. The world population of the Corvidae exceeds that of any other family.

This is not so in the Dominican Republic. Both of our species have diminishing populations, particularly the White-necked Crow, the one that lives at lower elevations. It suffers more from the impact of people than does the Palm Crow, which prefers to live in the piney woods.

Corvus leucognaphalus was first known to science from Puerto Rico in the year 1800. It was first reported from Santo Domingo in 1857, by La Salle (Proc. Zool. Soc. London, 1857 p. 32). It was considered endemic to Puerto Rico *and* the Island of Hispaniola. However, there has been no report of the bird from Puerto Rico for almost 20 years, thus making our island the only place where it is still known to exist. The White-necked Crow was very common in many localities as late as 1950, but since that time it has disappeared from the larger part of its range.

Many people consider that crows are destructive and that they consume the larger part of the corn and rice crops. They are also believed to bring bad luck and are associated with the devil. Many people think they are doing the country a favor when they kill these birds. Crows are hunted and used as food and are also used as a target for improving the aim of hunters from the upper class. Unfortunately the hunters and target-shooters do not think of the large quantities of noxious insects that crows can consume, nor that the birds have a role to play in the balance of nature.

The White-necked Crows are very interesting to observe. A courting pair kept me entertained for many hours one spring day when we had an outing along the River Mahomita, near the mountain village of Cacao.

We were resting a bit from a hike along the river, when two large black birds flew into a huge strangler fig tree. Paying no attention whatsoever to us, they preened, pecked at each other, fed each other, and conversed. But when one started to sing, I was sent into gales of laughter. The croaks, squawks, clicks and clacks were very expressive, and one could detect the urgency and pleading.

Under it all I could detect an interesting rhythm that suggested a melody, but it came out as a raucous, hoarse noise.

During the whole day I did not see one act of copulation. Was the ritual of courtship just beginning? How long does it last?

It is true what people say: that crows live by their wits. One day in the vicinity of Las Arenitas, on the northeast side of Hispaniola, we came across a large band of crows being pursued by several different species of birds. Palm Chats, Gray Kingbirds, a Black-cowled Oriole or two, and a small hummer were chasing and pecking the larger birds. It was obvious that they were dive-bombing and flapping their wings in violent protest against the presence of the crows.

The group passed quickly and, as they flew out of sight, I noticed one lone crow flying out of a Palm Chat's nest, with a nestling in its beak. It had taken advantage of the ruckus to carry out a robbery and gain a meal.

One week in April, in 1976, we were camped close to the Parque National de los Haitises, in an area called Arroyón. We were studying the Ridgway's Hawk by day and listening for the song of the Stygian Owl at night. It was there that I had the scare of my life.

It was my turn to keep nocturnal guard. I had my station prepared with care: a chair to sit on and a blanket to wrap around me to keep out the damp, chilly, night air of the jungle. Close at hand I had a water jug, a flashlight, and a small table that held the recording equipment. I even had an extra battery for my hearing aid. As soon as it was dark my husband went to bed and I was alone at my post.

The first few hours were fairly pleasant as the sky was clear and the lightning bugs were giving the stars some good competition as they flitted, flew, blinked, and twinkled around me. I wondered just how many species we have on the island. The click beetles had their double headlights turned on and glowing; the blue-green light was so bright I could read the letters printed on the buttons of the tape recorder. A solitary cricket sang a lonesome tune, and the tree toads chirruped. I tried to count species. Suddenly I became so sleepy that I laid my head down on the edge of the little table for just a minute.

Voices brought me back to consciousness. I hardly moved except to turn up my hearing aid. Someone was speaking in a language that I couldn't understand or recognize. It wasn't English, nor Spanish, nor Patois. A voice was very insistent, another answered. Another sounded like the whining of a child. Then there was a commotion and the sound of running. That started up a series of new voices, some low coos, clicks and clucks, then some conversation. Just what language were they speaking, anyway? How could I make someone understand that I, with all my various gadgets, was an old, harmless birdwatcher recording owl songs? I hoped no one would pass my way; I felt very uneasy and finally decided to call my husband.

He woke with a start when I touched him.

"Listen," I said softly. "Listen!"

He listened carefully, then put on his shoes, grabbed the flashlight and walked out into the open.

"I'd feel more secure," I said apologetically, "if I could understand their language."

"Stay here," he commanded, as he took off in the direction from which the sounds were coming. After a while he came back, laughing fit to kill.

"Your people," he said, "are goats. A whole flock of goats. A billy and several nannies and one of them is in heat."

That explained one series of voices but not the coos, clicks, clucks, and conversation. By that time, though, the noise had stopped, and my husband took his turn at the listening post while I went to bed.

We didn't hear any owls that night.

The next day I found out that a flock of White-necked Crows had roosted not far from our camp. A man came by and asked what we were doing. When I told him about recording the songs of the birds, he asked me if I had heard the crows conversing during the night. He said they make lots of noise when they are courting! How foolish I felt! Goats and crows were my suspected intruders!

The White-necked Crow is not easily distinguished from the Palm Crow *(Corvus palmarum)*. Although they are known to live side by side they are not often found together, making it difficult to make comparisons in the field. The white feathers on the neck of *Corvus leucognaphalus* are not visible unless the bird is in the hand, making that characterization of little use, and size is hard to judge. The vocalization, however, is diagnostic. The Palm Crow is much more vociferous and gives one simple sound, raucously repeated: *"Cow, cow, cow."*

Palm Crows are much more aggressive and audacious than the White-necked Crows. They often follow an intruder for as much as a mile, flapping their wings and screaming, *"cow."* They even make daring, darting forays toward a person.

I consider the Palm Crow misnamed. Since its preferred habit is the Pine Forest, it should have been called the Pine Crow.

Both crows are seen in the Dominican Republic, but you must know where to look for them. One must travel from 1½ to 2 hours to get to a place where they MAY be seen.

In Haiti, however, the White-necked Crow is very common around Port-au-Prince, where there are trees, and at an agricultural experiment station at Damian. The birds are not bothered there, since the Haitians are not allowed to have guns.

A Messenger from Eden

The La Selle's Thrush

Order:	Passeriformes
Family:	Turdidae
Scientific name:	*Turdus swalesi*
English name:	La Selle's Thrush
Spanish name:	Zorzal de la Selle,
	Cho-Cho

Have you ever seen a black bird the size and shape of an American Robin that has a bright orange bill, a chestnut-colored upper breast, a deep, flame-colored abdomen with a wide, white median line? I would easily win a bet that you have not, because very few people have. It is the rare La Selle's Thrush, *Turdus swalesi*, that inhabits only the dense, humid forest of some of the highest mountains on the Island of Hispaniola.

The bird was first discovered on the Massif de la Selle, Haiti, in April 1927, and later described by the late Alexander Wetmore of the Smithsonian Institution in Washington, D.C. It was not recoreded elsewhere until 1971, when the author and her husband were exploring for orchids in the Baoruco mountains back of Barahona, on a mountain called Pie Pol.

We had a difficult time finding Pie Pol. We had to make several trips before we were lucky enough to locate it. One day in May, 1971, we had the good fortune to meet up with an old rancher who owned a coffee plantation. He told us that the mountain was known on the map as Noche Buena, but after the death of Trujillo its name was changed to Pie Pol. It didn't take us long to find the people who owned the property. We found a guide and made our camp beside a group of shacks that are used by coffee pickers during the harvest.

We started out early in the morning, setting a good stiff pace because the rainy season had already begun and we wanted to get to the summit and down again before the usual torrential downpour started about one o'clock. It would be nip and tuck to make it, because the clouds were already hanging low over the area.

We walked through a coffee forest, beautiful and fragrant with the white flowers of the third and last flowering of the coffee trees. Even though it was early, bees hummed, birds sang, crickets chirruped. We took time out to stop and hear and smell and see everything. Even so, we made good time in the half-light of the early dawn, and by nine o'clock we had passed the last of the plantations and were on our way into the virgin forest.

The *campesinos* had planted beans and corn right to the line where the "manacla" palms started. We entered an opening and immediately began creeping through a tangle of fallen trees, ferns, wild ginger, creeping bamboo, and flowering plants like begonias, gesnerias, and some terrestrial orchids. We crawled, jumped, pushed, and squeezed ourselves through some very precarious places. We were wet to the skin from the fog and the dew. After about 20 minutes we came to an opening but could see no trail. We were cold and discouraged. Then the guide found us a trail of sorts, the fog lifted a bit and the sun broke through. We could see the tops of the tall trees. They were so old, they were completely covered with mosses, anthuriums, bromeliads, peperomias, philodendrons, orchids, and ferns of all sorts and descriptions. Everything was festooned with lianas that hung down like ropes between the trees. The ground was like a sponge. When we walked the moisture oozed out, and a fetid odor of decomposing vegetation filled the air. Then we noted a peculiar, orange-colored glow, not unlike an aurora borealis. It was caused by the sunshine reflecting on the dozen, maybe a hundred blossoms of the bright, apricot-colored orchid, *Neocogniauxia hexaptera*. Against the deep green of the dark forest, the area looked like something out of the land of fairies.

While we were feasting our eyes on a once-in-a-lifetime phenomenon, our guide told us in a low voice, "I see a black Trogon." Knowing that our Hispaniola Trogons are not black, I hurriedly searched for the bird at which he was pointing. Oh, glorious day! I recognized it at once. It was the La Selle's Thrush, the rare *Turdus swalesi*! I was seeing it for the first time in my life, and it was a new record for the Dominican Republic.

We were overjoyed when our bird was joined by its mate, and one of them sang its never-to-be-forgotten spring song. Although we searched the area for a long time we did not find its nest. In fact, to this day no one else has ever found a nest in the Dominican Republic.

We have seen and studied the La Selle's Thrush in other areas of the Baoruco range. In Zapotén, near Aguacate, we recorded its bubbling, rollicking song, and watched it feed at daybreak on the ripe, wild strawberries that grow in the grass at the edge of the trails that lead through the pine trees. In Loma de Toro we obtained a specimen. We caught one in our mist net and found that an adult weighs about 110 grams.

We looked again for its nest without success. In Las Abejas, near Canotes, I saw it preening on an old stub in a dark, humid canyon that was dripping with moisture from a recent rain. In Pueblo Viejo, one hopped unconcernedly through our camp. Once I sat for 45 minutes in a glade of a mixed forest festooned with vines, mosses, and ferns where I saw the bird feed on earthworms. In the Sierra de Neiba we saw a pair carrying food to their young, and although three of us looked for its nest for three full days we were unable to find it.

In 1977, a *Turdus swalesi* was caught in a mist net by some bat hunters above Convento on the road to Valle Nuevo in the Cordillera Central. I have some unverified reports of its presence on the trail to Pico Duarte.

No one has ever seen the La Selle's Thrush below 4,500 feet in elevation. Since its discovery in 1927 by Dr. Wetmore, the destruction of its habitat in Haiti is practically complete. Did it always live in the high mountains of the western part of the Dominican Republic, or has its range shifted eastward due to the disappearance of the proper habitat in Haiti? I am sure that its instinct to survive could have led it to the Dominican side of the mountain ranges. But still, its secretive ways and timid nature could have caused it to be long overlooked.

One of my most memorable experiences was the time in April, 1978, near Zapotén when I saw a La Selle's Thrush sitting on a high branch of a pine tree silhouetted against a lemon-yellow and orange sky, pouring forth its evensong as an Angelus.

Note: In December, 1986, Dr. Gary Graves and Dr. Storrs Olson of the Smithsonian Institution reported that the La Selle's Thrush found on the Cordillera Central and the T. swalesi from the Sierra de Baoruco were different. In recognition of the contribution made by the author in the discipline of ornithology in the Dominican Republic, the sub-species is called Turdus swalesi dodae.

A Very Endemic Bird

The Palm Chat

Order:	Passeriformes
Family:	Dulidae
Scientific name:	*Dulus dominicus*
English name:	Palm Chat
Spanish name:	Cigua Palmera

The Palm Chat *(Dulus dominicus)* is the State Bird of the Dominican Republic. The people could not have chosen a better species to represent our unusual island.

It is certainly distinctive. The ornithologists had to create a new family for it, and it is the only member of its family. Its closest known relatives are the Waxwings and the Silky Flycatchers, but even the tie with those two groups is very distant. The early scientists changed its name seven times before it was agreed that it should be *Dulus dominicus*. Only since 1975 have we known for sure that it had no relatives. The egg white proteins and the blood analysis studies conducted by Dr. Charles Sibley of Yale University proved beyond any doubt that the bird is unique. Therefore it must have originated on the Island of Hispaniola, since it does not live any other place in the entire world.

The Palm Chat is easily recognized. It is about eight inches in length and of drab coloration. The upper parts are greenish brown, the lower parts are yellowish white, heavily streaked with brown. The feet are gray, and the eyes are red. The sexes are similar as are the juveniles, but sometimes the young ones are slightly darker than the adults. In the field the adults are distinguishable only by their larger size.

The bill and the feet are worthy of special attention; both seem to be adaptations to the peculiar life-style of the species. The bone-colored bill, which is heavy and slightly curved, has a noticeable ridge, the upper mandible overlapping the lower one. The lower mandible has an indentation or a shallow trough at its base. This slot is convenient for carrying the twigs that are used as material for the nest. The feet are particularly large for the size of the bird. They are clearly helpful in nest construction.

One of the most interesting and unusual things about the bird is its nest. It prefers to build in the Royal Palm, but if there is none available, then any other kind of tree will do, provided it has a long trunk and high branches. Sometimes the nest encircles the crown of a palm, using the lower fronds as a support. Others are placed around the trunk on the flower stalks a bit below the crown. The entire nest is made of twigs measuring from 10 to 18 inches in length; occasionally a twig will reach 20 inches. Normally the structure is about the size of a bushel basket, but at times it takes on gigantic proportions. That is when we find other species taking advantage of the top of the big pile of twigs. We have seen a pair of Greater Antilleans Grackles nesting on the roof, using it as a platform for its own structure. We have found a pair of Ridgway's Hawks in Los Haitises using the roof of the Palm Chat's nest in like manner.

At first glance, the nest looks like the work of a pack rat, with the twigs thrown every which way. But if you were able to look inside you would find that it is organized as a condominium. There are four or five separate, shallow nests woven from strips of palm leaves that look like the bottom of a basket that has an over-under weave. There are side entrances that give some privacy to each pair, but there is a tunnel that connects the nests to give incubating birds a way to communicate and visit.

Apparently the nest site is chosen to be placed close to trees with a good supply of dry branches that produce pencil-sized twigs. Then the band goes to work gathering material. A twig is grasped in the beak and with a wrenching motion it is broken off. Once in a while, if the twig is too thick or not dry enough, it does not break. Then the bird tries another tactic. It grasps the twig in its beak and jumps downward, using its weight to break the twig. If the twig falls it is again seized in the beak and carried crosswise to the nesting site.

Some birds, which could be young ones with less experience, lack the ability to measure the twig size. They have trouble breaking the twig in the first place. Sometimes, after it is broken, it becomes entangled in the larger branches of the tree and the carrier loses its balance and has to start over.

I have seen Palm Chats carried downward while trying to transport a twig that is too heavy. The bird seldom drops the twig, but when it does fall, it is retrieved and arranged in a better position until the bird can fly upward again.

The birds are continually carrying twigs. One has to observe for some time to see if they are making a new nest or repairing an old one. One gets the impression that a Palm Chat just cannot pass up a good-looking twig.

The nest seems to be the social center. The owners not only nest in the structure, they sleep in it and use it as a shelter from both the sun and the rain.

Two to four eggs are laid in the individual nests. These have a bluish-green background that is heavily scrawled and blotched with a purplish brown color that gives them a very dark appearance.

When the young are fledged, they and the parents make up the band, which numbers from 16-20 individuals. They perch together, sleep together, search for food together, and feed together. A few hours of following a feeding flock can often result in obtaining some unusual information. It will certainly prove to be highly entertaining.

The Royal Palm *(Roystonea hispaniolana)* is probably the favorite tree, as it provides a good location for the nest, some of the nesting material, and food. Both the flowers and the fruit are taken. Then there is the Guano Palm *(Cocothrinax argentes)*, the Caya Colorado *(Bumelia salicifolia)*, the Penda *(Citharexylum fruticosmum)*, and the Almacigo *(Bursea simaruba)*, as well as other wild fruits. I have seen a young bird almost choke to death trying to swallow an entire blossom from a Majagua tree *(Hibiscus tiliaclus)*. Occasionally I have seen the Palm Chat hawk for insects, but this kind of food does not make up a large percentage of its diet.

While feeding, the Palm Chats converse noisily with a large variety of semi-musical notes. When I listen to them, I always wish I could understand bird language. What are they saying to each other? Do they always live together in harmony as they seemingly do? Does any one member of the band stand out as a leader?

They seem to have a highly developed sentinel system. If there is an intruder, a very loud call is heard, "Cheer, cheer, cheer, cheer." The flock immediately becomes quiet, and nothing moves. Then a loud *"Sush-shush-sush-sush"* is given. Within a short time the entire flock leaves the tree from the opposite side from where they were first seen.

The Palm Chats show a social concern for each other. If one individual happens to be some distance away from the crowd, very soon a member of the group will go perch by it, getting as close as possible. As soon as they are settled, a second bird appears and sits close, often touching the perching bird. Still another comes, and another, until the branch is crowded. They push and shove until there is quite a commotion, and I have seen the first bird actually pushed off the end of its own perch!

The Palm Chat is not offensive nor is it destructive in either its nesting habits or its feeding practices. But like every other bird on the Island of Hispaniola, it is hunted and killed and used as food.

The Palm Chat is abundant and widespread in the lower elevations, seldom going higher than about 1,500 feet. It does not live in the pine forests. It is most common in the areas of higher rainfall but also lives in dry regions. There are several large populations in Santo Domingo, in the Zoological Park, and a particularly large number live in the National Botanical Garden. And, you may even see them from your hotel window!

Once a birdwatcher made a special trip to the Dominican Republic to see our strange, endemic bird. He was nearing the end of his stay and getting desperate. He had not been able to identify the *Dulus dominicus* and therefore called the Museum of Natural History for help. We made arrangements to meet at the entrance to the Botanical Garden. As luck would have it, he arrived first. While waiting he observed some birds in the trees outside the gate.

When I arrived he said, "What is this drab bird I am seeing? It seems to live in groups and is very ordinary."

"You are seeing the famous *Dulus dominicus*," I answered.

"*Dulus dominicus* in the city? I have been seeing it all week in the palms by the hotel and I didn't recognize it? I thought it was rare and beautiful!"

He sounded disappointed. The Palm Chat may not be rare and beautiful but it is one of the strangest birds in the world. It lives only on the Island of Hispaniola and on the two small islands just off the coast: Gonâve and Saona.

How much longer will the Palm Chat be abundant? How much longer will their bands enjoy life among our Royal Palms? The destruction of habitat, too much uncontrolled hunting, and the menace of the brood parasite, the Glossy Cowbird *(Molothrus bonariensis)* are certainly factors that can make drastic changes in any bird population. We can only hope that the Palm Chat is numerous enough and widespread enough to be able to withstand these problems.

The Ghost Singer

The Rufous-throated Solitaire

Order:	Passeriformes
Family:	Turdidae
Scientific name:	*Myadestes genebarbis*
English name:	Rufous-throated Solitaire
Spanish name:	Jilguero

The Jilguero or Rufous-throated Solitaire is a thrush, and like so many other thrushes it is best known for its song. Invariably, if its name is mentioned someone will remark, "Oh, yes! I know that bird! It whistles just like a person but it is very hard to see." Because the bird is heard and not frequently seen, it is often called the "Ghost Singer."

The Jilguero begins to sing before dawn, even before the day breaks. It is the last one to become silent at nightfall. But the best concerts are given on the dreary, foggy days when it is so dark and so cold that the bird seems to feel lonely and sad, and is singing to keep itself company. The weird, woeful, minor notes are combined to make interesting variations that live long in the memory of the person who has been privileged to hear them.

The whistle is a simple, prolonged *"tweet"* that sounds like a fiddler drawing the bow across the strings of a violin. Immediately following the *"tweet"* there are three or four *"tu-tu-tu"*s, all on the same note. Less frequently a series of three clear notes, one low, one high, and one in-between, is produced. At times it would seem that the bird has become tired of singing; then the last note becomes a buzz. The song is easy to imitate, and what fun we have had trying to "bring it in." There is always an answer, but the name of the game is to locate the singer after you have heard the song.

Since the Solitaire is most often heard singing from a high branch of a tall tree, it would be easy to think that this is a typical habitat, but this is not so. We have seen it at only three meters from the ground, feeding on ripe poke berries (Moco de Pavo, *Phytolacca rivinoides*) and the fruit of the Palo Amargo *(Colubrina berteroana)*. We have caught it in the lower trammels of our mist nets, and the young run along the ground in a robin-like manner. It seems that this species ascends to the higher levels only to broadcast its declarations to the world.

To see a Solitaire one must have very sharp eyes and a large measure of good luck. It is quite useless to start searching for it when it begins to sing because it is still too dark to see. About 8 o'clock the bird begins to look for food, and when a low bush or tree laden with fruit is found it generally stays close by until it has had its fill. Many times it is so occupied with eating that it fails to pay much attention to an intruder.

Scanning often brings results if you are in the proper environment. The Solitaire is capable of sitting perfectly still for several minutes. If you look in a moderately tall tree, be it broadleaved or pine, you may see one if you look close to the tree trunk and behind the leaves.

You will see a beautiful bird if you are lucky. The Rufous-throated Solitaire is about eight inches in length, with a longish tail and a flat-appearing head. It is mostly gray, darker on the upper parts and pale gray on the under part. There is a bright, rufous red spot on the throat and another of the same color on the under-tail coverts. The chin is white; there is some white on the wings and tail, and a white spot at the side of the beak. The white eyelids combine to give the bird a glowering facial expression.

On March 7, 8 and 9, 1975, we found Jilgueros near the Hotel Montana in Jarabacoa at an elevation of 500 meters. It was the first time that we had found them at this elevation. Generally they live at the higher elevations and only at times during the cold season do they descend to lower levels. But the birds we found there were in breeding condition, indicating that they could live in lower elevations also. The Jilguero has such a varied diet of seeds, fruit, and insects taken on the wing, it seems that it could easily adapt to both elevations. Since the bird is not particular about its nesting site, this would be another factor in its favor. It will nest in banks, creepers that cover a large stone, a hole in a tree trunk, or in the middle of a fern or bromeliad. It uses various kinds of weeds that are shaped in the form of a cup. Two or three spotted eggs, tinged with blue, are laid.

One day in November, 1979, after the hurricane *David* we were hunting orchids in the Cordillera Central near Siberia close to Constanza. The fruit-eating birds were enjoying some over-ripe berries on a Palo Amargo tree. The Stripe-headed Tanager and several Solitaires were having a great time chasing each other as they competed for the fruit. Wintering warblers added a note of color and interest to the scene, and I was royally entertained for several hours.

After a while I noticed something strange was happening to the birds. They flew less and less, and some fell off their perches; others would try to change positions and miss the mark. Finally it dawned on me! The berries must be fermented.

147

I was certain they were after I saw a Solitaire trying to sing. The bird sat on a small branch, hunched up with its feathers fluffed out. The beak moved, but I heard no sound. The bird appeared to go to sleep, but jerked its head up when it was about to fall. It tried singing again. The *tweet-tweet-tweet* came out, but the *tu-tu-tu* was muffled and dwindled off in a descending note that faded away completely, and then the songster fell. The tall ferns broke the fall, and again the bird flew up to its perch. Then the process started again. I watched for a long time before I was called. I often wonder how long it was before the little fellow was overcome by sleep!

We have seen this species in all the main mountain ranges of the Dominican Republic, including the Cordillera Septentrional, and have heard it sing in the higher parts of Los Haitises. The Rufous-throated Solitaire also lives in Jamaica, Dominica, Martinique, Santa Lucia, and Saint Vincent. It does not live in Puerto Rico, and Cuba has its own endemic species.

A Very Different Vireo

The Flat-billed Vireo

Order:	Passeriformes
Family:	Vireonidae
Scientific name:	*Vireo nanus*
English name:	Flat-billed Vireo
Spanish name:	Ciguita Juliana

The Island of Hispaniola seems to have more than its share of puzzling endemic birds. The tiny *Vireo nanus*, discovered as new to science in 1885 by William Cory, had its name changed several times before it was finally classified correctly. It was first called an Empidonax flycatcher, and remained with the flycatchers for many years, but placed in a new genus. More studies revealed that it was out of place as a flycatcher and it was listed with the song birds in 1907.

Not until 1917 did the scientists have enough specimens to make an adequate study, but nothing was published although the bird was reported to be a vireo. In 1927, Dr. Alexander Wetmore conducted a thorough investigation of the bird and found it to be a vireo beyond the shadow of a doubt, but it had a very peculiar bill. It was broad, depressed, and triangular in shape, whereas other vireos have a slightly decurved bill with a small notch. For that reason, when Wetmore presented his findings at a meeting of the American Ornithological Union in 1927, he called the bird a "Flat-billed Vireo."

The Flat-billed Vireo is pretty, prim and pert, quick-tempered and flighty, with a very aggressive personality at times. Its peculiar behavior makes it a most entertaining bird to observe. The song is distinctive, and if it were not for its vocalization, it might easily be overlooked because it is an excellent example of protective coloration and is very difficult to see. It has greenish-olive-gray upperparts, whitish lores, and a whitish ring around the eye which accentuates the light eye color. The wings are darker, with faint whitish margins and with a broad band of white across the primary coverts, making a definite wing bar. The bird can be either white or light yellow on the underparts. It is about 4½ inches long.

Our first contact with the Flat-billed Vireo came about when we explored in the area of Monte Palma, at the foothills of the Sierra de Baoruco, in February, 1973. We carefully made our plans to go with our friend, Sandino, who had a plantation of beans on the mountain. We were curious to see how a crop could grow in a semi-arid region; we wanted to see some new and interesting habitat and to study the birds and orchids as well.

"It is a long way to my *parcela*, Sandino said. "But if you are here at my house at 4 a.m. about February 15 when the moon is right, we can make a good trip. The hardest part of the trail is on the hill back of us. If we can make it to the top by daybreak, the rest of the way can easily be done in about three hours. The hottest, hardest part we can do while it is cool."

That sounded like a good plan, and we told him we would be there on the set date. Actually we came a day early and spent the night in his patio near the goat corral. We retired early to escape the mosquitoes and to be well rested for the journey. We woke up when the cocks began to crow. We made coffee and ate a light breakfast, made ourselves a lunch, and then looked at the skies while Sandino loaded the mule. We had two saddle bags, "hárganas," made out of Guanito palm leaves; the bags were filled with our little butane stove, food for three days, extra clothing, sleeping bags and plastic ponchos in case of rain. Each of us carried our toilet articles, a flashlight, water, and binoculars. It looked as though we were going to have an adventure.

We were excited, and felt fresh and cool in the early morning. The moon was bright and the sky clear; we found various constellations, the Southern Cross, and the planets. Just when things were beginning to get interesting, Sandino yelled, "¡Vámonos! There is no time to look at the stars!"

We hit the trail about a quarter of a mile from his house. The going was rough. The trail was steep and narrow, and we had to walk over rolly rocks. The mule didn't like his load and had to be coaxed. He made several unexpected stops, making it difficult for us who followed. The creeping cactus called gauasávara seemed to jump at us, and the thorn bushes grabbed at our clothing. Finally Sandino became impatient with the mule and delivered him a resounding whack on the rear that sent him flying up the hill. We had to use the flashlights every now and then when we had to walk under the shade of a tall treee, but we made good time. And, as Sandino had predicted, we were at the top of the hill by daybreak.

The rest of the trail was quite routine and comfortable. It had been a logging road years before, therefore it was wide and not exceedingly steep. We were in Sandino's *guandule* patch in time for a late breakfast, made over the one-burner stove. Afterward we unloaded the mule and set up camp in a lean-to made of stakes and banana leaves. That was our center of operations.

We immediately set out to study our surroundings. We found a hillside of second-growth bush, cambrón trees, cactus, and many little coulees or *arroyos*, some with larger trees and more brush. There we looked for orchids and saw a goodly number of our common birds, mostly migratory warblers and the Greater Antillean Bullfinch. We saw a Red-tailed Hawk and a few pigeons, and collected several orchid plants. It was late afternoon when we returned to camp.

We had to move fast to get our supper and make up our beds in the open. It gets dark early and fast in the tropics in February. The clear sky looked fascinating, but we stayed awake only long enough to hear a Barn Owl screech and to hear the plaintive call of the Pitanguá.

Imagine our surprise to be awakened by the rain falling on our faces. It was a fine, drizzly, soaking rain that didn't last, so we were not bothered much. On the contrary, it was helpful. In the morning hours the insects and the birds were out in full force, The whole place seemed to explode with bird songs.

We were very busy for a while identifying birds. Suddenly my husband spotted something he had never seen before. He came to my side, saying, "Come and help me identify this bird."

"What kind of a bird is it?" I asked.

"I don't know. That is why I came after you," he said softly. "Come over here with me."

After I located the bird in my binoculars, I said, "It is some kind of flycatcher." We hurried to consult the *Field Guide* and looked up flycatchers. It said absolutely nothing about the bird that we were seeing; we both agreed that it must be something new.

The tiny bird was very accommodating. It was soon joined by another one, and although they flitted around a lot, they stayed pretty much in the same area. We chased them around most of the day, listening to their conversations and the song, *"Wheet, wheet, wheet."* We noted all the essential characteristics to make a good description and we recorded the vocalizations. It had no particular melody, but we thought it was fly-catcher-like. I could hardly wait to get back home to tell someone of our luck.

The pair was still around the next day, so we decided to put up a net. We caught 14 bullfinches, several common yellow-throats, several yellow-faced grass quits, and not a single new flycatcher. By the time we had to break camp, my fingers were sore from being pinched by the bullfinches and one Black-crowned Palm Tanager. I was glad to take the net down.

We had no problems on the return trip. The mule had a lighter load, and we started back after the heat of the day had passed. But we were ready for a bath and a meal by the time we reached Sandino's goat corral.

The insects were terrible. We decided to go further down the road and find an irrigation canal to bathe in, since our water supply was practically exhausted. It didn't take us long to find a good, secluded place, not far from the main road. We took our towels, soap, and fresh clothing, and made our way over the rocky road.

"Last one in is a fathead," I called as I shed my dirty shirt and trousers. But I shed no more. The mosquitoes began to bite, and they came in swarms zinging around our semi-naked bodies. We jumped, danced, and grabbed for our clothes, and after running to the sanctuary of the car we finished dressing. What could we do? We had to have a bath!

We filled the big jugs with canal water and drove up out of the mosquito zone. There we heated the chilly water, bathed, ate supper, and went to bed. We went to sleep immediately, and all was well until my husband yelled, "I've been bitten! There's a scorpion in my bed!"

He felt it crawl across his hand and turned the flashlight on it, then gave his hand a fling. The insect must have been thrown through the air and down on the floor of the car, because it didn't bother us again all night. However, we were too tired to care much. We went to sleep again almost immediately, not even waiting to rub the sting with garlic. The next morning I found a dead scorpion on the floor of the car when I swept up after breakfast.

Not long after our trip to Monte Palma our friend Dr. George B. Reynard came to Santo Domingo to care for an experimental plot of tomatoes. We proudly told him of our new flycatcher. We played the recording we had made, but he did not recognize it. We promptly suggested that he take it back to the States and consult with someone at the Academy of Science, or meet with Dr. James Bond, author of our *Field Guide*.

Within a few days we received an answer. "The recording is the song of the *Vireo nanus*."

We were a bit disappointed, to say the least, but after we did some research work in the *Smithsonian Bulletin*, #155 (1931) by Wetmore and Swales, we were happy to know that we were not the only people who had been fooled. The same characteristics that had confused the early ornithologists had confused us too.

The Flat-billed Vireo is far from being rare in the Dominican Republic, but it does have a specialized habitat. It is found only in the dry, scrubby places, frequently where there are outcroppings of karst limestone. It shuns the high mountains and the pines. We have seen it along the coast at the Boca de Cumayasa, and the Boca de Yuma on the southeastern coast of the Dominican Republic. We have seen it on the north coast near Puerto Plata, and by Monte Cristi, and in the semi-desert area of the Northwest. We saw a pair on the road to Padre las Casas, and there is a good population near Puerto Escondido and in the *arroyo* back of La Descubierta, near Lago Enriquillo. Both the National Park of the East and the National Park of Los Haitises have good-sized populations.

Once, when we were working in the foothills of the Baoruco mountains on the southern side of the island, near the town of Enriquillo, we made camp in a very dry forest with tall, decidious trees, lots of underbrush, and much leaf mold. There were charcoal makers present, but by following goat trails through the woods we found some very interesting things. We visited a cave where we collected an abundance of owl pellets for analysis and study. We saw a Rosy- breasted Grosbeak there, and a Blue Grosbeak as well. A very mysterious hummingbird that had a royal purple head and a shimmering white crown attracted our attention. Later that same day, I saw a small gray and white hummer, both never to be seen again.

That same trip I found a small nest in the shape of a cup, newly constructed, made of horsehair and fine, dry grasses, slung between two small branches (forked) in a low tree of the underbrush of the forest, about 100 yards from the main road. Since it was on the middle part of a limber limb and only about five feet from the ground, I could pull it down to see inside. It was empty, but looked clean and new. I thought that I would surely find the owners around somewhere. I found a convenient place to sit and wait as I felt a *Vireo nanus* would show up sooner or later. My patience paid off because in about ten minutes I heard the now familiar song, *"Wheet, wheet, wheet, wheet,"* and the answer. The pair came working through the underbrush, gleaning insects from the underside of the leaves of the lower story. They were never far from the vicinity of the nest, and I didn't have to move to keep them in sight.

I stayed there until my stomach told me it was time to eat. I made my way back to the car and started preparations for lunch, and sat down to wait for my husband to come. As I sat enjoying a slight breeze, I heard voices and soon a burro with two boys astride came down the road. Both youngsters were armed with slingshots.

As they passed the car I spoke to them, and they sniffed the air. I guess the smell of the food reminded them that it was time to eat because the bigger boy, seated on the burro's haunches, gave a jump backward and landed on his feet in the middle of the road. He turned his head to one side as if listening for something, then took off up the trail. He was back in a flash, threw an object to the younger boy still seated on the burro, then jumped back on. Then the feathers began to fly.

I started after them, yelling, as they went. "You have killed my birds! You have killed my birds!"

"And we are going to eat them," said the larger boy.

He continued picking the feathers from the tiny body, greenish gray feathers mixed with yellow ones. And when he finished, he popped the body just as it was into his mouth and chewed. The small boy did likewise.

I was horrified. I was dumbfounded. I opened my mouth to speak but I could not.

"One has to eat," said the smaller boy. Then he gave the burro a clout with his heels, and they bounced off down the road.

The Flat-billed Vireo belongs to the White-eyed Vireo complex that lives in the Caribbean. Each island has its own endemic species. We believe there are times when we have seen the migratory White-eyed Vireos from other islands, but so far we have not been able to distinguish species. We have recorded different vocalizations and have noted variations in color. But still, these may be only age differences, or light and dark phases in the life of the bird. We are quite sure that the young have brown eyes. Only a prolonged study can give us detailed answers to some of our questions about our fascinating, endemic, flat-billed, white-eyed, and flycatcher-like *Vireo nanus.*

It took us a long time to find out the Spanish common name for our peculiar bird. It is most interesting to know that the Dominican *campesinos* called it the Ciguita Juliana because they felt it was a relative to the Julian Chivi (the Black-whiskered Vireo). All the early scientists with their many studies and classifications took 42 years to come to the same conclusion!

A Shady Character from the Forest Floor

The Ground Warbler

Order:	Passeriformes
Family:	Parulidae
Scientific name:	*Microlegia palustris*
English name:	Ground Warbler
Spanish name:	Ciguita Coliverde

Because of its shy and retiring habits and its protective coloring, this little warbler is very difficult to see. It seldom makes a cheep or a chirp. It can't even attract attention with a song. It creeps along on the mossy branches or trunks of the broadleaf trees where the vegetation is the thickest and stays quite close to the ground. It seldom flies higher than one's head. The best way to observe it is to sit in a dark place in a jungle and be patient until one passes by.

However, if you do happen to find a nice, mossy log that looks comfortable, look well before you sit down. Sometimes old wood harbors a few undesirable residents, like centipedes and scorpions. Both are poisonous but not fatal, the sting of the centipede being the worst. I have had a few narrow escapes that still make me shiver when I think about them.

Other creatures can be studied, too, while you wait for the Ground Warbler to appear. The many species of spiders are active, and are varied in color, size, and shape. Their webs, when laden with moisture or dew, make wonderful subjects for photographers. (You need not worry about seeing tarantulas. They are mostly nocturnal and they are not plentiful in damp, cool places. They like a dry, hot climate much better.)

There are various species of moths and butterflies, beetles and flies, that are extraordinarily beautiful. But it behooves one not to lose interest in the bird...it blends in so well with the environment, you are apt to miss it if you are not careful.

The first thing to be noticed is the broken eye ring; it stands out like a small light until the bird moves. Then you notice the gray head, the mossy green of its back and tail, then the gray underparts. Sometimes, if you are close enough, you can see the red eye.

The nest of the Green-tailed Ground Warbler is made of fine grasses; it is cup-shaped and placed in a bush or shrub. The nests I have seen generally have had a few gray feathers placed here and there. Two pale greenish spotted eggs are laid.

During the breeding season the bird has a feeble song, a simple *"sip-sip-sip."* It sits on an outside branch of a low bush or a blackberry vine and sings with its whole body as well as its voice. The *sis-sip-sip*, all on the same note, is rendered indefinitely. Sometimes this warbler also emits a sound like a small bird in distress, but I do not understand under what conditions this peculiar behavior takes place. One day, on December 28, 1982, we heard that cry on the road to Aguacate. We looked for nearly twenty minutes before we found the author in a tangle of berry vines and underbrush.

The Ground Warbler is seen in many environments: at sea level, at the Boca de Cumayasa, at the Boca del Río Soco, in the Parque del Este, in the arid forests of Azua, and in the cut-over lands on the way to Padre las Casas, but it is most common in the gray-green, misty mountain areas of the Cordillera Central and the Sierra de Baoruco. To me, this indicates that the Ground Warbler lived at one time all over the island and now has adjunct populations. Many species must always have cover and when the forest is cut away, they become prisoners of their own environment.

The Warbler that Turned into a Tanager

The White-winged Warbler

Order:	Passeriformes
Family:	Parulidae
Scientific name:	*Xenoligea montana*
English name:	White-winged Warbler
Spanish name:	Ciguita Aliblanca

The endemic White-winged Warbler of Hispaniola *(Xenoligea montana)* has been and still is a scientific mystery. Ever since it was discovered by R.H. Beck on January 15, 1917, there have been questions about its identity. It was described by Chapman *(Bull. Amer. Mus. Nat. Hist.* Vol. 37, May 14, 1917, p. 33). It was given the name of *Microligea montana*. It was reported from Haiti by Bond *(Proc. Acad. Nat. Sci.,* Philadelphia, Vol. 80, 1928, pp. 513-14). Lonnberg reported it in 1919, and Moltoni obtained a specimen in La Maguana *(ATT. Soc. Ital. Scienz Nat.,* Vol. 68, 1929, p. 324).

There was nothing new reported as to its life history by Alexander Wetmore in 1931 when he studied the structure of the bird. In Bulletin #155, p. 397, he says, "This species differs structurally from *Microligea* in a much heavier bill and less fluffy plumage. Though Wetmore is inclined to consider from his personal experience that the two species under discussion belong in different genera he is not at this time prepared to separate them since, except as noted above, *palustris* and *montana* appear identical in structural characters."

In 1967 James Bond wrote in his Thirteenth Supplement to the *Check-list of Birds of the West Indies*:

> I feel compelled to use the name *Xenoligea* proposed as a subgenus for *Microligea montana* as a generic name of this wood warbler. My reasons are (a)that I consider *Xenoligea* more distinct than many currently recognized genera of this region and (b)that Dr. George H. Lowery, who is co-author of the parulid section in a forthcoming volume of *Check-list of Birds of the World* informs me that *Xenoligea* will be given full generic rank.
>
> As stated in the Twelfth Supplement, *Xenoligea montana* differs from *Microligea palustris* by its shorter and thicker bill and more compact plumage. *X. montana* has considerable white on both remiges and rectrices, and is more arboreal than other species of this complex.

As far as I know there have been no further studies made on *X. montana.* We have searched diligently to find its nest, hoping that when its biological history is known some light would be shed on the true identity of this species. But for the very reasons that the bird is unique, it is also a difficult bird to study. It lives in an environment above 5,000 feet, where there are definite seasons of the year. The breeding cycle of this forest-dwelling species coincides with the rainy season. During these months the roads are impassable, and travel in a jeep or a VW bus is done at the risk of life and limb. Even so we have made many forays into the mountains looking for the bird's nest. We have seen such new and beautiful country, and have enjoyed ourselves immensely, but we have had no success in solving the mystery of the life history of the White-winged Warbler.

My first contact with the White-winged Warbler came during a camp-out in Zapotén in April, 1970. Zapotén is a Haitian name that did not have any meaning for us but over the years came to mean the best place in the world to find birds. There are so many ecosystems and mini-ecosystems within such short distance of each other that we have been able to record 47 species just sitting still and letting the birds come to us.

Loma de Toro, where Zapotén is located, is in the Baoruco Range on the southwestern side of Hispaniola. The International Highway, which is the boundary line between Haiti and the Dominican Republic, is steep, with much rolling rock and always in poor condition because there is little or no maintenance. To get to Zapotén you leave the main Carretera Sánchez at Duverge and drive over a new road to Puerto Escondido. This is an arid, irrigated piece of flat land that boasts of a population of maybe 500 people, a military outpost, a forestry service, and an irrigation project that obtains its water from a small river called Las Damas. Driving west from the pueblo you cross the flat and start slowly toward Aguacate. On this road we have found many ornithological treasures: a band of Cedar waxwings that are seen only every 20 years or so, Kentucky warblers, a pair of Trogons living in the desert, flocks of Hispaniolan Siskins some distance from the pine forests, and the Bay-breasted Cuckoo. The uncommon Greater Antillean Night Jar is common here, and we have recorded the song and calls of the Least Pauraque.

In the *arroyo* just before you get to Aguacate, the military outpost, the Pitangua can be seen and heard *(Caprimulgus cubanensis)* and the Potoo *(Nyctibius jamaicensis)* has been seen. We were able to seé the Potoo fly over the camp and perch on an old stub, and although it was in plain sight it was hard to distinguish it from the dead limb.

At Aguacate the *militares* always stop us, to pass the time of day and to tell us the condition of the road. For security reasons they want to know if we are going through or if we will camp out. Then we move on to Zapotén.

Zapotén is a wide, flat place on the righthand side of the road, about 5,180 feet in elevation. At one time a sawmill was located here, but it was closed down in 1967. There are still many spots of virgin forest that are beautiful beyond description. There are pine trees on the ridges, mixed forests of broadleaf trees on the hillsides and a lot of brush, ferns, creeping bamboo, aspen, parrot trees, cuba trees, and wild fruit trees in the *arroyos*. Under the grass, in the areas where the pines were cut, there are wild strawberry vines. Here we have seen nearly every species that dwells in the high mountains: hawks, night jars, migratory warblers, Trogons, Chat Tanagers, the rare and beautiful La Selle's Thrush. One year a colony of Purple Martins nested in a dead pine tree. We discovered that it has a delightful spring song.

One cold morning about 4 a.m., when we were camped at Zapotén, we were rudely awakened by the call of a Barn Owl that sang right beside the car. What a lucky break for us!

We noticed the eerie greenish light of a moonless sky and wondered why everything was so bright and clear. What a thrill it was to discover the brilliant, unmistakeable Bennett's Comet above the southwest horizon!

Late in the afternoon of our second day in camp we found an indignant White-winged Warbler in our mist net that we had placed along the road above our camp. Because it was a dark day and late as well, it took us a while to disintangle our captive. By the time we had freed it from the net it had lost most of its tail feathers. Nevertheless I can still describe it.

This beautiful little bird is about 5½ inches long. The back and wing coverts are a lightish moss-green. The head and the tail are gray; the lores are black with a white spot on either side of the forehead. The wing feathers are black with a prominent white streak on the primaries. The underparts are immaculate white, as are the outer tips of the tail feathers. The "white streak" on the wing serves as a field mark but it has caused a certain amount of confusion. In Bulletin #155 (Smithsonian Institution, 1931, Wetmore and Swales), the late Alexander Wetmore wrote, "There is a white spot on the wing which becomes a streak." It seems that many people remember the first and see the spot, not the streak. And during the late summer we find some birds with a yellowish cast to the underparts. (I consider these to be young birds.) I have had many people confuse the White-winged Warbler with the young male *Dendroica caerulescens*. In winter this bird is a gray-greenish blue on the back and head, with light underparts and a white spot on its wing.

By studying the stomach contents of the few specimens that we have obtained, we discovered that the bird consumes a great many small insects, but during the winter season when there is a scarcity of insects in the higher elevations the bird feeds on the small seeds of the "Cuba" tree *(Trema micrantha)*. In Bretón as well as in the Sierra de Baoruco, the birds have earned the name of *Cubera*.

I had never heard the White-winged Warbler utter a sound until we recorded a few soft notes during breeding season (Record, "Bird songs of the Dominican Republic," Cornell University, Laboratory of Living Sound). It wasn't much of a song—a *"sip"* or two with a good deal of wing flaps. I was very disappointed, to say the least.

We have made many trips to the mountains to look for its nest but we have not been successful. We do know that it nests in the area of Zapotén because we caught this species in our mist nets and some of them looked very shop-worn as if they were brooding. But we never found a nest.

Early in 1989 Mara McDonald from the Smithsonian Institution informed me that the White-winged Warbler is now classified as a tanager. Studies had been made using the DNA system.

The Bright, Dark Queen of the Forest

The Stripe-headed Tanager

Order:	Passeriformes
Family:	Thraupidae
Scientific name:	*Spindalis zena*
English name:	Stripe-headed Tanager
Spanish name:	Cigua Amarilla
	(in the Dominican Republic)

The *Spindalis zena* is found throughout the Caribbean area. There are many geographic variations in its color and patterns; even on the Island of Hispaniola the birds differ from one mountain range to another. Nevertheless they are all considered to be one species.

Although *Spindalis zena* is neither rare nor endemic, and it does not lay claim to being a great songster, it deserves a place in the hall of fame for its beauty, stateliness, and majesty. It has many common names throughout its range: Orange Bird, Cabrero, Reina Mora, Spanish Quail, Goldfinch, Red Robin, and the Tom James Bird, the most appropriate being Reina Mora, which means Wild Queen.

The male is easily identified. It is from six to eight inches long, and is a symphony of contrasting but harmonious colors. The head is mostly black with wide, white supercillary and malar stripes. The underparts are bright yellow, the breast washed with brilliant orange. The black wing feathers are margined with white. The female, however, is not showy. She is typically olive green, darker on the upper-parts. The Hispaniolan race has the rump and the upper tail coverts yellowish, with the underparts indistinctly streaked. The females of all the races have some white margin on the wing feathers. It is easy to identify immature males, but the young females may cause problems.

One would expect this beautiful bird to have a song, but that is not the case. It has a rather weak warble in the springtime, but it is seldom heard. In all the years that I have known the *Spindalis zena*, I have heard it sing only once. That was during the month of April in Monte del Estado, close to the town of Maricao, in Puerto Rico. The song could be written as *"tse, tsee, tsee,"* all on the same note. The call note is nothing more than a faint *"seep."*

In the Dominican Republic the Cigua Amarilla inhabits the forests and shrubbery of the mountains. I have never seen it below 2,500 feet except in the interior of Los Haitises. However, in Puerto Rico and other parts of the West Indies it lives at sea level as well as in the higher mountains.

The diet of the Cigua Amarilla is varied. Some insects and large quantities of berries from the parasite "El Conde" are taken, as well as poke berries, wild blackberries, strawberries, and some weed seeds. During the time when it is cold and food is scarce in the mountains, I have seen them eating fermented fruit from the Palo Amargo trees. This has an interesting effect on the bird's behavior. Some birds become belligerent in defense of their food supply, others are unable to control their flight, and others try to sing.

Once, in July, 1974, when we were camping out in the southern mountains near the Hole of Pelempito, we found a young *Spindalis zena* that had fallen out of a nest located in a tree near the camp. The nest was a small cup made of grasses and dry material, loosely constructed.

The young bird could not yet fly. We searched in vain for siblings; knowing that this species lays two or three eggs, we thought we might find some close by. Evidently the rest of the offspring had fledged. When we examined the unfortunate little fellow we discovered it was suffering from the warble fly and several larve were ready to come out.

This parasite was probably responsible for the retarded development of the little one. Since nature in the wild does not favor the weak, the fledging was probably abandoned. After we returned the little creature to the ground under the nest, its piteous cheeps did not continue long. I am quite sure that a mongoose had found an easy meal.

A Resourceful, Common Tanager

The Black-crowned Palm Tanager

Order:	Passiformes
Family:	Thraupidae
Scientific name:	*Phaenicophilus palmarum*
English name:	Black-crowned Palm Tanager
Spanish name:	Guiro, or Cuatro-Ojos

The Black-crowned Palm Tanager may be described in one word: ubiquitous. It is found in every kind of environment from sea level to the highest mountains; it lives in the xerophytic forests as well as humid rain forests and those that lie in between. It lives in open country as well as in woodlands. Basically, it lives anywhere that food can be found. Its diet, consisting of fruits, seeds, and insects is so varied that it can easily find food anywhere.

Its nesting habits also help the bird. The nest may be situated in a number of places: in vines, on a bank, on an abandoned tractor wheel, or in a tree. It is a rather haphazard affair made of dry grasses and twigs, cup-shaped, moderately deep and rarely lined. Two or three whitish-green eggs are laid.

Normally the Black-crowned Palm Tanager has not much of a song. It has a nasal-like *pe-u*, frequently given as a means of communication with its mate. But in the springtime, just at dawn, a thin, high-pitched melody is heard. The rhythm is reminiscent of the song of the Chat Tanager, but with a remarkable difference in pitch and volume! You must be alert to hear it, but once heard it is something you are not likely to forget.

We have often caught the Black-crowned Palm Tanager in our mist nets, and what work it is to get them out! If you catch one, you catch its mate. The first one to be caught protests so violently with its distress signals that the second one always comes to see what has happened. The birds are very pugnacious as well as active; it takes a long time to entangle them. My poor fingers have bled from the peckings of the long, sharp, heavy beak.

One day when we were exploring near the northwestern coast in a place called Buen Nombre we came to a moist canyon on a hillside where we found many pairs of the Black-crowned Palm Tanager. We had hiked a long way and before turning back we decided to sit on some rocks and rest for a while. We were sitting close to an almacigo tree full of ripe fruit, and before long the birds were flying all around us.

First we saw the Gray Kingbirds and the Greater Antillean Bullfinches, then came the migratory warblers that were after the fruit flies. A Piculet flew in and shortly afterward its mate came. There were woodpeckers, the Black-whiskered Vireo, a mocker or two, and some Red-necked Pigeons. As we watched, a pair of Black-crowned Palm Tanagers joined the crowd.

We sat still for quite a while and my neck was beginning to ache, because the almacigo tree was very tall. When I changed my position I inadvertently kicked a rock loose and it went rolling and tumbling down into the gully.

With a thump it hit the almacigo tree-trunk and of course it frightened the birds away. Everything flew except a screeching Black-crowned Palm Tanager. It was hanging down, with a foot caught in a dangling vine.

The cries became urgent, full of distress and fear. Soon a second tanager appeared and joined in the vocalizations, but suddenly it stopped screeching and perched on an open branch opposite the unhappy, captive bird. It seemed to be sizing up the situation. Then it began to converse in a calmer voice. The entangled bird became a little more assured and stopped struggling so violently. The free bird hopped to the branch from which the vine was hung and coaxed the captive until it flew up and perched beside the free one. Together they picked at the vine; then one would rest for a while as the other worked. Finally the foot was free.

I thought I detected a note of real joy in their "Guiro" as they flew away, down into the *arroyo*.

The Black-crowned Palm Tanager is one of our most beautiful and common endemic birds. It is almost seven inches in length. Its upper parts are yellowish green and the head is a shiny black with three immaculate white spots on the face—one above the eye, one below the eye, and one in the back of the beak. These give the bird the appearance of having four eyes, hence the Dominican name Cuatro-Ojos. The underparts are gray except for a white throat patch.

In Haiti there is a Gray-headed Palm Tanager reported by Bond as common in the Kenscoff area above Port au Prince. One day while working on the south side of the Baoruco Range, we thought we saw this specie in the Dominican Republic. My husband secured several specimens but each one turned out to be juveniles of the Black- crowned species. Not until 1982 did he see that Gray-crowned species in and around the Massif de la Hotte.

The Problem Birds from the Island of Hispaniola

The Chat Tanagers

Order:	Passeriformes
Family:	Thraupidae
Scientific name:	*Calyptophilus frugivorus*
English name:	Chat Tanager
Spanish name:	Chirrí

Our sunrise service on an early, frosty Easter morn in the Sierra de Baoruco had its own private choir. *"Chirri, chirri, chirri, chip, chip, chip."* The clear, cardinal-like notes of the Chat Tanager rang out from the deep *arroyo* below our camp and the woods vibrated with echoes. The author of the song expressed a great deal of determination and power in its rendition, making it a strong challenge to the whole world in general.

I recognized the song from the description in the book *Birds of the West Indies* by James Bond, but I still had not had the pleasure of seeing a Chat Tanager. After hearing it, I knew I just had to see it and so dedicated a full day to a Chat Tanager hunt.

We scrambled through underbrush, crawled through creeping vines, and walked through leaf mould so deep it felt like stepping on sponges. We sat still and waited, we climbed hillsides that looked like walls, we hunted until we were wet, cold, and hungry. The frustrating thing about it all was that the bird kept singing at regular intervals throughout the entire day, but we were never able to find one. It was a game of hide-and-seek, but we were always the losers.

It took us a full year, with much patience and persistence, before we finally made progress.

We were again camped at 5,800 feet at Zapotén, in the Loma de Toro, beside the same deep, dark canyon, all set about by broadleaf forest. Most of the canyon floor and the side hills were covered with small pine trees, blackberry vines, and creeping bamboo. We were once more greeted by the Chat Tanager's song.

This time we were prepared. We recorded its voice, then we played the tape. What a response! I played it about three times and we heard the now familiar *"Chirri, chirri, chirri, chip, chip, chip."*

Out of the heavy brush flew a middle-sized bird, bearing a strong resemblance to a mocker: long tail, heavy bill, and spreading wings. It landed on the lowest branch of a young Palo de Viento tree and sang its full song. The bird, evidently a male, appeared to be agitated or angry. The tail jerked, the wings were somewhat spread, the head came up, and the beak opened and closed. At first glance you see a dark body with a darker head and an immaculate white throat patch. Then, once it moves, you could see that the underparts are white and the body is chocolate brown. (It also has a yellow spot on the bend of the wing and on the lores; these spots are not visible while in the field.)

We were so completely captivated that day by the personality of the Chat Tanager that ever since then we've made it a special project to select camping places where we were reasonably sure of seeing one.

In one of our trips to Chat Tanager country, a "real" ornithologist was part of our investigation team. He wanted to see the elusive bird, too, and guaranteed us the use of his mist net so we could capture one and have a close-up view. We stretched our nets in likely places and played the tape but to no avail. Unfortunately the bird did not cooperate with us by singing on that trip, because we were well into the month of October and the courting days were over.

Sometimes it is a great temptation for a person to embroider on or to fabricate reports when the competition gets rough and one would like to be at the head of the line in seeing "firsts." On our last day in camp, I was loudly lamenting that I had not seen a Chat Tanager up close. Our friend said, "Oh, I saw some early this morning. I was walking up the hill when I heard bird noises. Right up ahead of me, around a shallow turn, I saw six Chat Tanagers feeding in the road."

I was green with envy, of course, but managed to congratulate him on his good luck.

Several years later, after I had become better acquainted with the habits of the Chat Tanagers, I realized that the story my friend had told me was completely untrue. How gullible and naive I was! You just don't see Chat Tanagers feeding in flocks in the middle of the road. They feed on the forest floor, eating centipedes, cockroaches, spiders, and the like. Their diet is about 90% insect matter and 10% vegetable. They are timid birds, staying under cover constantly, and they fly only short distances to cross a road or to move up a bank. They live in pairs, otherwise they are practically anti-social.

When we discovered the cañadas in the pine forests of the high altitudes we had better luck with the Chat Tanagers. This habitat is not only an interesting one, it is beautiful and unique. The cañadas are found mostly in the Sierra de Baoruco now, since that area

173

lacks water for agricultural development and the soil is so thin it does not serve for crops.

It is so cold during the greater part of the year, no one wants to live there; therefore, there is less habitat loss and very little people impact.

Cañadas are deep, dark *arroyos* where rain water has been trapped and, because of the density of the vegetation, the moisture is preserved. Aspen and a gymnosperm called Palo de Cruz are a few of the predominating trees, the latter having roots that cannot penetrate the rocky soil. These roots grow in grotesque shapes and forms on the surface of the forest floor and are covered, sometimes completely, with a greenish-brown moss that harbors all kinds of epiphytic plants: peperomias, anthuriums, gesnarias, orchids, and bromeliads. Then there are the ferns and several other species of moss, all of them making the cañadas virtually a natural botanical garden. In these places lives the food supply of the Chat Tanagers and the La Selle's Thrush.

One morning very early, before daylight, I ventured in a cañada alone. Really, there is nothing to be afraid of since we have no poisonous snakes or big wild animals on our island. An occasional wild pig with little ones could cause trouble, but mostly they do not stay around people. Still, I have to admit that it is an eerie feeling to be all alone in a cañada. The early morning breezes blow the mist and the fog in and around the moss-covered trees, making the festoons swing and wave like gray-brown ghosts. The damp cold penetrates your very being, and you become stiff and uncomfortable. The silence is deafening, and your imagination works overtime. You get claustrophobia, you want to get out to the light. Just as you decide to go, you see movement in a moss-covered bush. You forget your fear when you see the tell-tale triangular patch of white. Sure enough! It is a Chat Tanager! Happy enough to see one when suddenly you spy another, you forget your fears. Your day is made.

The bird hesitates. Then it drops like lead to the forest floor. It begins to scratch, making the leaves fly. Then, with a lurch, it reaches for something with its heavy bill and gobbles it up on the spot. Meanwhile, the second member of the pair has flown ahead and is also working in the leaf mould. In this manner the pair works through the forest.

One day we caught a pair in a mist net. It was early in the morning and right outside the cañada. We could see the yellow spot on the lores and the yellow at the bend of the wing. It was a *Calyptophilus tertius*, according to Dr. Wetmore, the one that inhabits the Baorucos. *(Birds of Haiti and the Dominican Republic*, by Wetmore and Swales. Bulletin #155, Smithsonian Institution, 1931.)

A month or so later we were camping on the Sierra de Neiba, to the north and east of Lago Enriquillo. We camped right by the International Highway, in a patch of virgin rain forest. Chat Tanagers sang all around us, but we noticed that the song was different from that of the Chat Tanagers in the Baoruco. It was the same pattern, but not nearly as loud. We put up a net on the north slope, not far below the military outpost.

About 15 minutes later we caught a Chat Tanager and we knew at first glance that it was new. The differences that we noted were in the size, color and, as mentioned above, the song. I think it apropos to reprint below the article about it that appeared in the May 25, 1977 issue of the "Notulae Naturae" of the Academy of Science in Philadelphia. I was very proud to have my name appear with that of James Bond, who had spent a lifetime working as an ornithologist in the Academy of Natural Sciences of Philadelphia, and who had specialized in the birds of the West Indies.

Here is the article by James Bond and Annabelle Dod, originally published in "Notulae Naturae" of the Academy of Natural Sciences, Philadelphia, May 25, 1977, to which the author refers above.

ABSTRACT.—A hitherto unknown form of Chat Tanager *(Calyptophilus frugivorus*: Thraupidae) was discovered in the Sierra de Neiba, Dominican Republic. The new race *C.f. neibae* is the smallest form of this species and combines characters of *C.f. frugivorus* and *C.f. tertius* (including *"selleanus"*) in a distinctive way.

Endangered and Endemic Birds of the Dominican Republic

A long abandoned section of the International Highway near the western border of the Dominican Republic has recently been reconditioned between Hondo Valle and La Descubierta on the northern shore of Lago Enriquillo. Taking advantage of this, the junior author explored the Sierra de Neiba, hitherto unknown ornithologically, her base a military outpost known as "Kilómetro 204" since it is that distance from Monte Cristi at the north end of the highway. The locality is over 5,000 feet above sea level, and is extremely humid with a dense growth of broad-leaf cloud forest on the north and south sides of the mountain, with scattered secondary growth and some pine elsewhere. Several species of considerable interest were encountered, including *Geotrygon caniceps, Turdus swalesi, Calyptophilus frugivorus,* and *Zonotrichia capensis.* The *Calyptophilus* is a well-marked undescribed race.
Calyptophilus frugivorus neibae subsp. nov.

Cory's *Calyptophilus frugivorus* mentioned in the article was from Cotuí, Pimentel, Samaná, and Villa Rivas. He made a statement in his book *Birds of Haiti and Santo Domingo,* 1885, p. 60: "All the specimens were taken in the swamps near Almercen, and none were observed elsewhere." This is considered incorrect by Alexander Wetmore, in *Birds of Haiti and the Dominican Republic.*

It is my opinion that the specimen taken later from La Vega by Abbott was *Calyptophilus frugivorus neibae* and not *C.f. frugivorus.* La Vega is a mountainous area; there is plenty of water but no lagoons. All the specimens that I have seen from the province of La Vega are *C.f. neibae,* and come from the mountains, where there are *arroyos* with water.

We have searched diligently near "Almercen" Pimentel, Villas Rivas, and in Los Haitises, and on the Peninsula of Samaná, but we have never yet seen the Chat Tanager described by Cory. The habitat destruction in that area has been unbelievable. Maybe this has caused the bird to become extinct. Since the Chat Tanager is primarily a ground dweller, it is likely that the slashing and burning farm methods and drainage projects have taken their toll.

Comparison of races of *Calyptophilus frugivorus*

		abbotti	frugivorus	neibae	tertius
Range		Ile la Gonâve	lowlands, N.E. Dominican Republic	Sierra de Neiba and (?) Cordillera Central, D.R.	Morne La Hotte, SW Haiti
Coloration	Upperparts	gray-brown	gray-brown with olive cast	rich olive brown	brown with olive cast
	Tail	pale gray-brown	olive brown	rufescent	rufescent
	Flanks & under-tail coverts	pale gray-brown to white	dull olive brown	sooty-brown	brown to rufescent
	Eye-ring	narrow, yellow	narrow, yellow	narrow, yellow	none or poorly defined
Size (males only)*	Wing (chord)	80.5-92.1 (87.1)	86-92 (90.4)	77-79 (78)	92.5-104.0 (98.9)
	Tail	78.0-95.2 (87.9)	81-89.5 (86.8)	83-85 (84.5)	96.5-108.0 (101.2)
	Culmen (from base)	20.1-21.3 (20.6)	19.5-21.3 (20.3)	20	22.6-27.4 (24.9)
	Tarsus	24.9-28.4 (26.6)	26.9-29.3 (28.0)	26-28	32.5-35.0 (33.4)

*Measurements in Wetmore, A. and B. H. Swales, 1931. *The Birds of Haiti and the Dominican Republic* (U.S. Nat. Mus. Bulletyin, 155) except *frugivorus*, 4 males measured by F.B. Gill, and *neibae*, 3 males measured by J. Bond.

The Clown of the Show

The Hispaniolan Siskin

Order:	Passeriformes
Family:	Fringillidae
Scientific name:	*Carduelis dominicensis*
English name:	Hispaniolan Siskin
Spanish name:	Canario

The colorful male Siskin of the pine forests reminds me of a tiny circus clown. It is dressed in a garb of greenish-yellow upper parts, bright yellow underparts, and a black hood. The bright yellow-orange of the bill contrasts sharply with the black face, making it a striking distinguishing characteristic. There is some black in the wings and the tail. The female is quite ordinary, being brownish-green with the breast streaked with palish yellow.

Both sexes are acrobats and can be very entertaining as they forage for food. They travel in small bands, feeding with the head down, balancing themselves on the slender stems of the wild, blue forget-me-nots of the alpine meadows. Or they flutter about the mature pine trees that are hosts for a parasite called Conde. Although many other species such as the Constanza Sparrow, the Greater Antillean Bullfinch, and the Pine Warbler are attracted to the Conde, I have never found the Hispaniolan Siskin in association with these birds. I often wonder if the Siskins augment their diet by eating the insects trapped in the resin of the pine trees?

It has been said that the Siskins like the pine forests and *are never found far from that environment*. We have found them a long way from pines, but where pines once grew. We take this as a good sign that the birds are adapting to other habitats. We have seen them near Angel Felix, on the south side of the Sierra de Neiba, near "K. 208," where the land has been cleared and is now open cropland. We have also seen them in Casabito, which has been practically denuded, and in Cortecito, above Monteada Nueva in the Sierra de Baoruco. But on Loma de Toro and in the hills back of Puerto Escondido, they are still numerous.

The Siskins are constantly on the move. As they travel, they converse and chatter. In the springtime they have a lovely, varied trill, often emitted on the wing.

The nest is a tiny cup of moss, situated in a low bush. There are two or three eggs, beautifully spotted with brownish. We found an empty nest in a sinkhole in the limestone hills of the Sierra de Neiba on May 25, 1977.

The Siskin was first found on the island of Hispaniola in the year 1867, near Port-au-Prince, Haiti. There were no specimens taken until 1881, when Cory visited the island. The first specimen taken from the Dominican Republic was secured by Donald Cherrie at Aguacate de la Vega and Catarrey in 1895.

This area around Catarrey has been deforested completely for many years, but in a recent period of reforestation, an effort has been made to replant pines. Will the little Siskins return? I do not think they will come very soon. They must have mature trees, with moss and parasites; a good ground cover of grass, and weeds. Bushes are also necessary for their life-style. Still, it will be interesting to observe what happens about 10-15 years from now!

Now Considered Endemic

The White-winged Crossbill

Order:	Passeriformes
Family:	Fringillidae
Scientific name:	*Loxia leucoptera*
English name:	White-winged Crossbill
Spanish name:	Pico cruzado,
	Periquito, Turquesa

In 1916 the famous ornithologist W. B. Abbott made a study trip to the Dominican Republic. In the course of his travels he arrived at the pine forests of Jarabacoa. Here the people of the area told him of a "Periquito" (little parrot) that lived high up in the pine trees and ate the seeds from the cones, breaking them open with a heavy crossed bill.

Immediately the ornithologist suspected something new. After searching for several days he collected one specimen near El Río, some distance from Jarabacoa but still in a mountain pine forest of the Cordillera Central. He identified the bird as *Loxia leucoptera*, an American bird from the far north.

In 1917 another ornithologist, R.H. Beck, found this species on Loma Rucilla and on Loma Pelona in the Cordillera Central, where he obtained 31 specimens. These confirmed the identification of Abbott, but more material had to be collected if adequate comparisons were to be made with other species of *Loxias*.

Because of political problems, nothing was done until April, 1927, when Dr. Alexander Wetmore explored the Dominican Republic and Haiti. He saw one crossbill in an open pine grove at an altitude of 2,000 meters in Morne La Selle in Haiti, and in May of that year the famous ornithologist made an extended search in the Great Valley of Constanza but had no success in finding the White-winged Crossbill.

James Bond reported that he had seen a flock of birds flying above the pines in the vicinity in which Wetmore had seen the Crossbills in Haiti, but he was not sure of their identification. It appears that he never saw this species in the Dominican Republic. Nevertheless, studies were made using only the collection of Beck, since nothing else was available at the time. The skins were compared with the skins of the other two forms, *Loxia bifascitta* of Eurasia and *L. leucoptera* of northern North America. It was obvious that all of them came from a common stock, but the crossbill from Hispaniola was given species rank, *Loxia leucoptera megaplaga*. Later, the birds were all considered *Loxia leucoptera* and the one from Hispaniola was given sub-species rank as *Loxia leucoptera megaplaga*. The differences are so miniscule that it was like splitting hairs to separate them; still, the widely separated geographic range had to be recognized.

It is difficult to explain the bird's presence on this island. Scientists say it dates back to Pleistocene times, 85,000,000 years ago. Were the Greater Antilles ever a part of the continental land mass of North America? Were the birds trapped here during some great geological upheaval? Have they always been migrants? No one could prove that they were a resident species because no one had ever found a nest on the Island of Hispaniola.

On April 2, 1971, while we were camping in the southwestern Dominican Republic in the Sierra de Baoruco (which is really an extension of the Morne de la Selle, the only known crossbill location in Haiti) I was attracted to pair of chattering crossbills. The female, carrying a small twig in her beak, flew right in front of me up to a branch about 15 meters high in a 20-meter pine. There I saw a mass of twigs that looked like the beginning of a nest about three meters from the trunk.

The habitat was open pine forest *(Pinus occidentalis)* at about 1,475 meters elevation. There were grasses, bracken fern, wild forget-me-nots, and other herbs, plants, and pine duff that sheltered patches of wild strawberry plants. The pines merged into denser, moist limestone broadleaf forest at the higher elevations, but there were no big pine trees as the area had been recently logged. (The sawmill was closed in 1967.)

The nest, probably in its first or second day of construction, was situated squarely on a main horizontal branch about five or six cms. in diameter and additionally supported by a projecting cross branch. At 10:30 a.m. the nest was a flimsy platform of woven twigs, lichens, and "Old Man's Beard." At the end of our three-day stay, the pair had transformed the platform into a reasonably compact, opaque, cup-shaped structure.

The female did the larger part of the work, many times rearranging or tossing out the material that the male had contributed. The male spent a large part of his time actively feeding, preening, or sunning himself on a nearby branch of a dead tree. We had to leave before we could make any further observations.

In a subsequent trip about two weeks later, we found the nest completely destroyed. It was probably razed by a Red-tailed Hawk or a Sharp-shinned Hawk got the young, because both were present in the area. The only thing to redeem my day was the gallon bucket of wild strawberries I gathered for making jam.

The color and number of the eggs of the White-winged Cross-bill is unknown in Hispaniola, as well as the period of incubation. This highly specialized bird is not numerous in Hispaniola. Maybe it never was, but the almost complete destruction of the pine forests of Haiti and the over-cutting in some of the high mountains of the Dominican Republic caused the loss of too much habitat to support a great population. However, since 1967 the sawmills in the Dominican Republic have been shut down, thus giving the birds a reprieve. In some areas, it has actually increased in numbers.

The birds are seen regularly on the trails to Pico Duarte and in the national parks of Ramírez and Bermúdez in the Cordillera Central. The former habitat around Constanza is now planted in potatoes, cabbage, and other cool growing vegetables. In the Sierra de Baoruco, it is seen around Zapotén and Loma de Toro, and in Pueblo Viejo, in the mountains back of Puerto Escondido, and in Canotes on the south side of the Loma de Toro.

The male White-winged Crossbill is a brilliant rosy red with black wings and tail. It has two white wing bars. The distinguishing characteristic, of course, is the crossed bill. The female is dusky, with the rump and the underparts washed with greenish yellow; her two white wing bars are quite conspicuous. The immature is blackish above, streaked with whitish, and the underparts are dusky white streaked with black.

Their vocalization is a soft *"Chu-chu"* or *"Shik-shik,"* repeated over and over. If there is a spring song, I have never been fortunate enough to hear it.

Dr. Cameron Kepler and Dra. Angela Kepler, ornithologists from Puerto Rico, were our guests during the camping trip when the nest of the White-winged Crossbill was discovered. As a result of our observations, an article about our find was written and published in *The Condor.*

Note: Recent studies in the Dominican Republic by Craig W. Benkman have proven that the White-winged Crossbill is endemic to Hispaniola (personal communication).

A Finch that can Pinch

The Greater Antillean Bullfinch

Order:	Passeriformes
Family:	Fringillidae
Scientific name:	*Loxigilla violacea*
English name:	Greater Antillean Bullfinch
Spanish name:	Gallito Prieto

The Dominican name for this species is Little Black Rooster. It is an appropriate name. The heavy cone-shaped bill and the manner in which the bird perches, erect and watchful, give the impression that it is always ready to pick a fight. Although the song is weak, an insect-like *"squichy, squichy, squeee,"* with a prolonged last syllable, the manner in which it is delivered adds to the notion that the author of the song has an aggressive nature and is willing to take on the whole world.

But these are first impressions. Study the bird for a while and you will discover that it is a series of contradictions. It is actually timid in its habits, always lurking in the vegetation for protection. It seldom flies long distances in the open. Although it does not attack other birds, it is powerful and capable of protecting itself. The beak is a weapon to be respected; just ask someone who has had experience with it!

Once when we were studying in an area called Palma Dulce, near Duvergé, we inadvertently put up our mist nets close to an abandoned pigeon pea plantation. In less than two hours we had caught 14 Gallitos. They were so belligerent and so expert in wielding the wicked beak that we had to take the nets down. My fingers were bleeding profusely. The bird is capable of pinching so hard that the blood will come through the unbroken skin.

The Greater Antillean Bullfinch lives in any kind of environment. It likes the broadleaf forests of the high mountains as well as the desert, the cut over lands, and the *arroyos* of the dry forests below sea level around Lago Enriquillo. Its food consists of seeds and small fruits, which are found abundantly on our tropical island. Sometimes insects are also taken.

The nest of the Gallito Prieto is variable in form. Sometimes it is located in a shrub, in the crotches of cactus plants, or in low branches of a tree of moderate size. It is globular in shape with an entrance at the lower side. The bulky structure is sometimes lined with vegetable cotton and thistledown. On some islands the nests are found now and then on the ground, and even in a hole in a tree, but on our island the nests are found in shrubs or trees. Three spotted eggs are laid.

The Greater Antillean Bullfinch is about six to seven inches long. It has rufous red eyebrows, a throat patch, and under tail coverts of the same color. The rest of the plumage is completely black. The female is just as beautiful as the male. She is brown with bright orange patches.

For a time some ornithologists thought there might be two species of this bird on the Island of Hispaniola. A thorough study was conducted in April and May of 1975 that proved there were no significant differences in different areas of the species's range, other than size.

The Greater Antillean Bullfinch inhabits the Bahamas, Jamaica, and Hispaniola, including the adjacent islands.

This bird is a victim of pesticides and polluted irrigation water, particularly in areas where commercial fertilizers are used.

A Misplaced Sparrow

The Rufous-collared Sparrow

Order:	Passeriformes
Family:	Fringillidae
Scientific name:	*Zonotrichia capensis*
English name:	Rufous-collared Sparrow
Spanish name:	Ciguita de Constanza, Pincha

I first identified the Constanza sparrow on Casabito mountain in the province of La Vega in April, 1967. A singing bird with its head lifted and the beak pointing skyward was perched on a high, dry branch of an old *palo de viento* tree, declaring its territory. The bird was not brilliant in color, but it was very striking because of the black facial pattern. It appeared to have a bridle. The pileum and the sides of the head were gray, streaked with black. It had a beautiful chestnut collar; the rest of the upper parts were olive-brown with black streakings. It had two narrow white wing bars. The throat was. whitish, with a conspicuous black band across the foreneck. The lower abdomen was whitish gray.

The song, a sprightly, clear but simple trill, was reminiscent of a child's noise-maker, *"Wis-wis-wis-wis, wiswiswiswiswis."* The bird sang several times before it noticed the intruders. Then it raised its crest, gave us an inquisitive look, and flew into the underbrush nearby.

The Constanza sparrow seems to be oriented to pine trees on the Island of Hispaniola. I have encountered them in the mountains in pine forests and mixed forests, and in places where pines once grew and where an occasional one is still to be seen. Casabito, at an elevation of about 1,400 meters, is the lowest that I've ever seen them. This widespread species must be a remnant of a population that was here before the Antilles broke away from the larger land mass that included both North and South America. It lives from the tropical to temperate zone, chiefly in the highlands down to Rio Negro, Argentina, and Chile. In the north it is found from Panama to Central America. In the Carribean it is common on the islands of Aruba and Curacao, but at sea level, a puzzling disjunction.

One weekend in late September, 1972, we made an expedition to Valle Nuevo in the Cordillera Central. We were very surprised to find so many Constanza sparrows: young, juvenile, and adults. They were in association with a flock of Pine Warblers, which were also abundant. The environment was very helpful for study—open pine forest on a large flat of easy terrain. There were grasses, blackberry vines, and occasional bushes of *Lyonia* (Queen's Tree, Palo de Reina) growing in very poor, thin-looking soil mixed with rock. A small creek ran to the east of the flat. Here we made our camp.

We went to bed shortly after 7 p.m. It was dark by that time and very cold. A bitter wind whined around us and we drew our thin wraps closer and closer about us. Finally we could stand it no longer. We crawled into our sleeping bags fully dressed except for our hiking boots. We were loath to expose ourselves to the cold by changing our clothing.

We hardly slept that night. We added a woolen blanket to the sleeping bags, we put on additional sweaters, but still we shivered and trembled. At last we drifted off into a troubled sleep. We woke up when it was daylight to find a white world. What a frost! I declared I would never come back to that frigid place again.

But when springtime came, the thought that I might possibly find the unknown nest of the Constanza sparrow made me willing to brave the cold. We arrived there again on May 28, 1973. Everything was green, and the Pine Warblers and the Constanza Sparrows were everywhere, and singing.

For almost three days we looked everywhere for the nest that we knew should be around somewhere. We walked through pajón (coarse grass) that grew high overhead. We crawled through berry vines and bracken ferns, we searched the low branches on pine trees. At night we shivered and doctored our chigger bites. At the end of the second day we were very discouraged, but we decided to give it one more try: if by ten o'clock the following day we had not found anything, we'd break camp and move on.

We were up and out early the next morning. We hiked up to the pine grove, and before long a mixed group of birds came twittering through the trees. We enjoyed every minute of the outing, but we didn't notice any birds that looked as though they were nesting: no bedraggled females, no brood patches. Nothing looked furtive. At 10 a.m. we gathered up our gear and started back to the car, giving up the chase.

Over on the west side of an old road we noticed a particularly lush plant of Lyonia. I saw a bird fly in. I tried to put my binoculars on it but couldn't locate it. And it didn't come out. So I told my husband to walk slowly toward the bush while I watched. He did, and just before he reached the bush, out came a Constanza sparrow. I rushed to where the bird had come from and in plain sight, I found the nest. There was one beautiful blue spotted egg and one newly hatched chick. Oh, that ugly chick was beautiful! It was completely.naked except for one long, dark feather or two on the top of its head. The eyes were shut.

The nest was a cup-shaped structure about ten cms in diameter on the inside, with walls about 2½ cms. high. It was made of lichens, moss, and pine needles, lined inside with fine grass. It was about two meters from the ground in the middle of a small, leafy branch. The branch was big enough to give the nest good support. Although the Constanza sparrow lives in bands, it is not a colonial nester. The female does most of the work in nest- building and incubation; the male helps with the care of the young. Incubation period is 11-15 days, beginning when the first egg is laid. The nestlings fly in less than 15 days.

For many years it was thought that the Constanza sparrow lives only in the Great Valley of Constanza (from whence comes its common name), but it is obvious that its range has been extended. Nevertheless we were completely surprised to find a well- established population of this species in the Sierra de Neiba Range, in the vicinity of the Army outpost at "204." In February, 1975, at 1,791 meters, we heard singing males and caught five in our nets that we had put up on the roadside in a dense growth of bracken fern. The soldiers at the outpost called the bird "Pincha." The Sierra de Neiba is right on the Haitian border; therefore it is reasonable to deduct that the birds live in Haiti, too, even though there has never been a previous record from that country.

The Constanza sparrow presents us with a few unanswerable questions: Where did it come from in the first place? Did it migrate from the Cordillera Central? It could have extended its range, but more than likely it has lived in that area for centuries without anyone knowing it was there.

An Ornithologist Sees More Than Birds

Solinodon paradoxus

A Curiosity of Hispaniola

A sudden gust swept across the dark mountainside, swirling the dry leaves and swaying the weeds that grew around the log I leaned upon. But when the weeds ceased swaying, two pinkish, petal shapes continued moving.

I studied them, something different to look at (my neck muscles ached after hours of watching the birds in the Dominican tree tops). Leaning closer, I saw that the pink petals were ears, and that the ears were attached to a brown body.

I actually pinched myself. This creature belonged in dreams, or in Wonderland. Body of a rabbit, petal ears, bare possum's feet, tail of a rat, and, all the while I watched him, rooting in the ground like a small pig. In all my life as an amateur ornithologist, nothing compared with this, my encounter with the Solenodon—a living relic, extinct elsewhere in the world millions of years ago.

We were on an orchid-study expedition to a mountain known as the Nalga de Maco (The Toad's Behind) in the Dominican Republic, near the Haitian border. We had climbed steadily for almost an hour when our guide stopped to survey the trail. There had been heavy recent rains; part of the upper bank had dropped away, leaving a slushy, muddy, uneven ribbon to serve as the trail beside a deep ravine. After one look, I declined to proceed.

My husband, reluctant to leave me sitting alone on a mountainside, insisted that I could "make it." I knew I could make it, too, but when I looked at the muck-filled chasm below, I decided to stay and watch birds. My companions proceeded on their orchid hunt.

At first the time passed quickly. Two foot-travelers carrying huge sacks of shelled corn were glad to stop and chat while they rested. We spoke of the destruction of the forest, the bad road—a result of erosion caused by the slash-and-burn agriculture—and the need to stop such practices. They agreed with me in principle, but said they still had to eat. Shortly after making that emphatic statement they went on, and I again became engrossed in the birds.

Plain pigeons *(Columba inornata)* were feeding on the fruit of a strangler fig tree, and I saw beautiful gray-headed quail doves *(Geotrygon caniceps)* on the ground below. I heard, but did not see, parrots and parakeets, a Hispaniolan Trogon *(Temnotrogon roseigaster),* and a Rufous-throated Solitaire *(Myadestes genibarbis).*

About 4:30 p.m. the fog came in, and the forest grew quite dark. In the tropics in February, it is totally dark by 6:30; the thought of walking down the hillside without a flashlight was unappealing. I felt lonely and wished the men would come back. Finally, I decided to leave a sign showing my husband I'd gone ahead. I made some arrows with dead tree branches and put rocks in the trail, then started down toward camp.

I came to another strangler fig tree that was tall as well as incredibly thick. A small flock of Hispaniolan parrots *(Amazona ventralis)* and a few parakeets *(Aratinga chloroptera)* made an earsplitting racket as they vied for the best feeding places on the branches. Migratory warblers fed on the little insects that gathered around fruit trees.

I looked at the birds through my binoculars until my neck muscles ached. Lowering my head to rest a minute, I spied an old moss- covered log that I could sit against and use as a prop. I continued to study in this more comfortable position, but after a while I put down the binoculars again. More fog had blown in, making it too dark for the moment to see well. That's when I saw those pink petal ears among the nearby weeds. The solenodon (a creature I had at the time neither heard of nor seen) had its head down and was rooting in the leaf mould on the ground.

I sat perfectly still. Then, carefully raising my binoculars for a better look, I found I was too close to see anything but a blur. I wondered why the animal, whatever it was, took no notice of me; evidently it was hungry and oblivious to anything but the search for food.

I walked from the log to get a better view. The creature climbed the rotted, tapered end of the log, then ambled leisurely along, partially hidden by grass, to where I had been sitting. Then it disappeared. In a minute the weeds and grass began to shake; it was making its way toward the base of a small tree close by. Finally I saw it, all but its face.

Flesh-colored, short, rounded, hairless ears; long scanty hair; short front legs; longer hind legs and heavy haunches—all combined to give it a most peculiar appearance. Its long, rat-like tail had a white spot at its base. "It must be an old animal," I thought, "to have sores on its tail."

For more than half an hour I watched it. Some part of its body was always visible, moving in rhythm with its rooting nose. After making several circles around the log the creature disappeared below the upturned roots, not once having acknowledged my presence.

When I returned to the capital I visited my friend, Dr. Eugenio Marcano, the well-known naturalist, I told him of my experience.

"Write it down, Mrs. Dod, write it down!" he cried excitedly. "To my knowledge, you are the first person with a scientific interest who has ever seen this animal in its native habitat long enough to observe any of its habits. When they have been seen in the daytime, it was only when they have been run out of their burrows by dogs!"

"What is it?" I asked in awe.

"It is called a jutia," answered Dr. Marcano, "a name given to it by the indigenous Indians of Santo Domingo. Its scientific name is *Solenodon paradoxus*. It is an insectivorous animal, endemic to our island. It is considered to be a relic of antiquity, and has not changed since Pleistocene times."

Dr. Marcano gave me an old book to read. The description of the solenodon fit my observation made in the half-light on the mountainside. The animal is about the size of a small rabbit. The ears are short, rounded, and hairless; it has small piggy eyes and a long, snout-like nose that is continually used in rooting for food. The rat-like tail is about the same length as its body, and has an albino spot at the base. It has coarse, hairlike covering on its body, very scanty about the head. Its hearing seems to be poor. The salivary glands seem to be highly developed. It uses its front feet as hands, and sits on its haunches as it eats its food!

I had observed all these characteristics except for the snout, which I never saw clearly.

Suddenly I had to know more about this extraordinary creature and I launched on a research project.

Solenodon paradoxus was first thought to be related to the tenrecs *(Tenrecidae)*, with a near relative living in Madagascar. Then scientists, on the basis of more study of fossils, said it was more closely related to the shrews. But now there is good evidence that *S. paradoxus* is related to extinct North American insectivores of the family *Apternodontidae.* Another species, *Solenodon cubanus,* which occurred in Cuba, is believed extinct.

We now know that the average solenodon measures from 18 to 23 inches, nose to tail. Recent investigators have found that the animal makes ultrasonic vocalizations—twitters, chirps, clicks, and sometimes soft squeaks. (For a time scientists thought its hearing was poor; now it appears that its hearing is really quite good. But the solenodon is so highly specialized and adapted to its niche, it need not pay attention to much from outside of it.)

I visited the agricultural experiment station in San Cristobal, where Dr. Ana María Ricart was studying the solenodon's diet and intestinal parasites, as determined from the excreta of a specimen they had in captivity for a few days. I looked at the creature and its offspring. Although in poor condition, already suffering from diarrhea and malnutrition, they were clearly the same species I had seen in the woods.

Shortly afterward, I learned that both animals had died, and that one man involved in the study had been severely bitten and was very ill.

In my travels into the interior, I question the mountain people about this living relic. Occasionally someone gives a snatch of information. They say it is brave because it bites the dogs that chase it out of its hole. It moves about at night and hides in the daytime. It lives in burrows among the roots of old trees, or in small caves in the rocks. They say it eats chickens, but will not eat in captivity. Once I met a young man who had kept a female and her offspring in a cage for several days. Not knowing the nature of its regular diet, the solenodons were offered ripe bananas and cooked rice and beans. Both animals died within a few days.

The solenodon is rare and, although protected by law from hunting and trapping, the population continues to diminish. It has been hunted indiscriminately for years to satisfy the zoos and universities that want specimens. Now, as the human population increases, the destruction of the solenodon's habitat gives scientists new cause for worry.

The traditional slash-and-burn agriculture still goes on at an alarming rate. Poor land that will not yield enough crops to justify its use is cleared for farming anyway. As a consequence, many *campesinos* live precariously. It is no surprise that a person ignorant of science, laws or ecology is willing to earn a little extra money by illegal hunting of solenodons.

Only recently our little animal has been given more protection. The Dominican Center for Promotion of Exportation, in cooperation with universities, scientific institutions, and the Division of Fish and Game, has put a stop to the exportation of all threatened and endangered species. Nevertheless, clandestine hunting still goes on. There are, and always will be, poachers and collectors tempted to own a curiosity and have it on display. Some people will sell anything for a price, and special permits can still be obtained to hunt solenodons.

If institutions, organizations, and individuals would refuse to buy or receive illicit goods, and would report offenders to the authorities, our solenodon would stand a better chance of survival.

We do not need more studies of these animals in captivity. We do need funding for field studies, and a corps of honest protectors to defend them in their natural environment.

Glossary

Agave, *or* Pan de Pajaro	A tropical species of agave whose flower is called bird bread by the country people of the Dominican Republic.
Bambu	Bamboo.
Barrancolí	A bird related to the kingfishers that makes its nest in a bank.
Bolo, bola	A ball or something that is round.
Campo	Open fields, the country.
Campesino, a	One who lives in the country.
Caño hondo	A deep gulley.
Canosa, o	White headed.
Canario, a	Canary.
Cambrón	One of several species of thorny acacia.
Carpintero, a	Carpenter (referring to the woodpecker).
Carpinterito, a	Little carpenter, little woodpecker.
Ciguita	A small bird.
Cigua	A medium-sized bird.
Ciguapa	A lengendary being on the order of a Yeti, Big Foot or the Monster of Loch Ness.
Cotorra	A parrot.
Cotorrita	A little parrot.
Diablotín	A big Devil.
Flautero	One who plays the flute.
Locrio de cigua	A stew made from the flesh of the Ciguas (birds).
Loro	Another name for a Parrot.

Maorita, o	A Dominican name for the Flycatchers.
Palo de Viento	A tree whose leaves quake in the wind (*Didymopanax tremulus*).
Papagayo	Parrot, used in the Dominican Republic as a local name for the Hispaniolan Trogon.
Pichon	A big nestling.
Plaintain	A large banana-like fruit used both green or ripe as a starch substitute.
Pomarosa	Rose Apple Tree.
Quisqueya	Indian name for the Island of Hispaniola.
Rio Limpio	Clean River. There is a village and a valley of that name.
Siberia	Name given to a very cold area in the high mountains of Constanza. During the winter months often there is frost, and ice forms on the edges of small streams.
Squamated	scaly.
Tody, Todies, Todidae	A family of birds related to the kingfishers, endemic to the Greater Antilles. Each island has its own species, but Hispaniola has two.
Torico	Little Bull. This name is given to the Least Pauraque because one of its vocalizations is its song, *Tor-rí- co*.
Vireo nanus	Scientific name for the flat-billed vireo.
Yautía	A starchy root plant related to the Elephant Ears used for food. (Very tasty in stews.)

Birds of the Dominican Republic

Codes: N: Nests   R: Rare   M: Migratory or Winter Visitor
        C: Coast   E: Endemic   I: Introduced

Scientific name	English name
Tachybaptus dominicus [N]	Least Grebe
Podilymbus podiceps [N]	Pied-billed Grebe
Pterodroma hasitata [N]	Black-capped Petrel
Oceanodroma leucorhoa [C]	Leach's Petrel
Phaethon lepturus [NC]	White-tailed Tropicbird
Pelecanus occidentalis [NC]	Brown Pelican
Sula leucogaster [NC]	Brown Booby
Sula sula [RMC]	Red-footed Booby
Sula dactylatra [CRM]	Blue-faced Booby
Phalacrocorax auritus [CRM]	Double-crested Cormorant
Anhinga anhinga [C?]	Anhinga
Fregata magnificans [NC]	Magnificent Frigatebird
Ardea herodias [N]	Great Blue Heron
Butorides striatus [N]	Green Heron
Florida caerulea [N]	Little Blue Heron
Bubulcus ibis [NI]	Cattle Egret
Dichromanassa rufescens [NCR]	Reddish Egret
Egretta alba [N]	Great Egret
Egretta thula [N]	Snowy Egret
Hydranassa tricolor [NC]	Tricoloured Heron
Nycticorax nycticorax [N]	Black-crowned Night Heron
Nyctanassa violacea [N]	Yellow-crowned Night Heron
Ixobrychus exilis [N]	Least Bittern
Botaurus lentiginosus [M]	American Bittern
Mycteria americana [NC—extinct?]	Wood Stork or Wood Ibis
Plegadis falcinellus [N]	Glossy Ibis

Eudocimus albus [N]	White Ibis
Ajaia ajaja [N]	Roseate Spoonbill
Phoenicopterus ruber [N]	Roseate Flamingo
Dendrocygna bicolor [NI]	Fulvous Tree Duck
Dendrocygna arborea [N]	West Indian Tree Duck
Anas platyrhynchos [N domesticated?]	Mallard
Anas strepera [M]	Gadwall
Anas acuta [M]	Northern Pintail
Anas bahamensis [N]	White-cheeked Pintail
Anas crecca [M]	Green-winged Teal
Anas discors [M]	Blue—winged Teal
Anas americana [M]	American Wigeon
Spatula clypeata [M]	Northern Shoveler
Aythya affinis [M]	Lesser Scaup
Aythya collaris [M]	Ring-necked Duck
Oxyura dominica [N]	Masked Duck
Oxyura jamaicensis [N]	Ruddy Duck
Cathartes aura [NI]	Turkey Vulture
Accipter striatus striatus [N]	Sharp-shinned Hawk
Buteo jamaicensis [N]	Red-tailed Hawk
Buteo ridgwayi [NER]	Ridgway's Hawk
Circus cyaneus [MR]	Marsh Hawk
Pandion haliaetus [M]	Osprey
Falco peregrinus [MR]	Peregrine Falcon
Falco columbarius [M]	Merlin
Falco sparverius [N]	American Kestrel
Colinus virginianus [NI]	Common Bobwhite
Numida meleagris [NI]	Guinea-Fowl
Aramus guarauna [N]	Limpkin
Rallus longirostris [N]	Clapper Rail
Pardirallus maculatus [N]	Spotted Rail
Porzana carolina [M]	Sora or Sora Crake
Poliolimnas flaviventer [N]	Yellow-breasted Crake
Laterallus jamaicensis [N?M]	Black Crake
Porphyrula martinica [N]	Purple Gallinule
Gallinula chloropus [N]	Common Gallinule, Moor Hen
Fulica americana [N]	American Coot

Fulica caribaea [N]	Caribbean Coot
Jacana spinosa [N]	Northern Jacana
Haematopus paliatus [NCR]	Common Oystercatcher
Charadrius alexandrinus [NC]	Snowy Plover
Charadrius semipalmatus [C]	Semipalmated Plover
Charadrius melodus [NC]	Piping Plover
Charadrius wilsonia [NC]	Thick-billed Plover
Charadrius vociferus [N]	Killdeer
Pluvialis dominica [MC]	American Golden Plover
Squatarola squatarola [MC]	Black-bellied Plover
Arena interpres [MC]	Ruddy Turnstone
Himantopus himantopus [NC]	Common Stilt
Gallinago gallinago [M]	Common Snipe
Actitis macularia [M]	Spotted Sandpiper
Tringa solitaria [[M]	Solitary Sandpiper
Tringa melanoleuca [M]	Greater Yellowlegs
Tringa flavipes [M]	Lesser Yellowlegs
Catoptrophorus semipalmatus [NC]	Willet
Micropalama himantopus [MC]	Stilt Sandpiper
Calidris canutus [MC]	Red Knot
Calidris melanotos [MC]	Pectoral Sandpiper
Calidris fuscicollis [MC]	White-rumped Sandpipier
Calidris minutilla [MC]	Least Sandpiper
Calidris pusilla [MC]	Semipalmated Sandpiper
Calidris mauri [MC]	Western Sandpiper
Crocethia alba [MC]	Sanderling
Limnodromus griseus [MC]	American Dowitcher
Tryngites subruficollis [MRC]	Buff-breasted Sandpiper
Steganopus tricolor [MC]	Wilson's Phalarope
Limosa haemastica [MC]	Hudsonian Godwit
Burhinus bistriatus [N]	Double-striped Thick-Knee
Larus argentatus [MR]	Herring Gull
Larus delawarensis [MRC]	Ring-billed Gull
Larus atricilla [NC]	Laughing Gull
Larus marinus [CMR]	Great Black-backed Gull
Gelochelidon nilotica [M]	Gull-billed Tern
Sterna forsteri [CMR]	Forster's Tern

Sterna hirundo [NC]	Common Tern
Sterna dougallii [NC]	Roseate Tern
Sterna anaethetus [NC]	Bridled Tern
Sterna fuscata [NC]	Sooty Tern
Sterna albifrons [NCR]	Least Tern
Sterna maximus [NC]	Royal Tern
Sterna sandvicensis [CMR]	Sandwich Tern
Sterna caspia [CM]	Caspian Tern
Anous stolidus [NC]	Noddy
Rynchops nigra [CRM]	Black Skimmer
Columba leucocephala [N]	White-crowned Pigeon
Columba squamosa [N]	Red-necked Pigeon
Columba inornata [N]	Plain Pigeon
Zenaida macroura [N]	Mourning Dove
Zenaida aurita [N]	Zenaida Dove
Zenaida asiatica [N]	White-winged Dove
Columbina passerina [N]	Common Ground Dove
Geotrygon caniceps [N]	Gray-headed Quail Dove
Geotrygon montana [N]	Ruddy Quail Dove
Geotrygon chrysia [N]	Key West Quail Dove
Amazona ventralis [NE]	Hispaniolan Parrot
Aratinga chloroptera [NE]	Hispaniolan Parakeet
Coccyzus minor [N]	Mangrove Cuckoo
Coccyzus americanus [N]	Yellow-billed Cuckoo
Coccyzus erythropthalmus [M]	Black-billed Cuckoo
Hyetornis rufigularis [NE]	Bay-breasted Cuckoo
Saurothera longirostris [NE]	Hispaniolan Lizard Cuckoo
Crotophaga ani [N]	Smooth-billed Ani
Tyto alba [N]	Barn Owl
Tyto glaucops [N]	
Athene cunicularis [N]	Burrowing Owl
Asio flammeus [N]	Short-eared Owl
Asio stygius nectipens [NER]	Stygian Owl
Nyctibius jamaicensis [NE?]	Potoo
Hirundo rustica [M]	Barn Swallow
Petrochelidon fulva [N]	Cave Swallow
Corvus leucognaphalus [NE]	White-necked Crow

Corvus palmarum [N]	Palm Crow
Mimus polyglottos [N]	Northern Mockingbird
Dumetella carolinensis [MR]	Catbird
Turdus swalesi [NE]	La Selle Thrush
Turdus plumbea [N]	Red-legged Thrush
Catharus minimus [MR]	Gray-cheeked Thrush
Myadestes genibarbis [N]	Rufous-throated Solitare
Bombycilla cedrorum [MR]	Cedar Waxwing
Dulus dominicus [NE]	Palmchat
Vireo nanus [NE]	Flat-billed Vireo
Vireo altiloquus [N]	Black-whiskered Vireo
Mniotilta varia [M]	Black-and-white Warbler
Protonotaria citrea [M]	Prothonotary Warbler
Helmitheros vermivorus [M]	Worm-eating Warbler
Parula americana [M]	Northern Parula Warbler
Dendroica petechia [M]	Yellow Warbler
Dendroica petechia albicolis [NE]	Mangrove Yellow Warbler
Dendroica magnolia [M]	Magnolia Warbler
Dendroica tigrina [M]	Cape May Warbler
Dendroica caerulescens [M]	Black-throated Blue Warbler
Dendroica coronata [M]	Myrtle Warbler
Dendroica pinus [M]	Pine Warbler
Dendroica pinus chrysoleuca [NE]	Pine Warbler de Hispaniola
Dendroica striata [M]	Blackpoll Warbler
Dendroica discolor [M]	Prairie Warbler
Dendroica palmarum [M]	Palm Warbler
Seiurus aurocapillus [M]	Ovenbird
Seiurus noveboracensis [M]	Northern Waterthrush
Seiurus motacilla [M]	Louisiana Waterthrush
Caprimulgus carolinensis [M]	Chuck-will's-widow
Caprimulgus cubanensis [N]	Greater Antillean Nightjar
Siphonorhis brewsteri [NE]	Least Pauraque
Chordeiles gundlachii [N]	Antillean Nighthawk
Streptoprocne zonaris [N]	Collared Swift
Cypseloides niger [N]	Black Swift
Tachornis phoenicoba [N]	Antillean Palm Swift

Chlorostilbon swainsonii [NE]	Hispaniolan Emerald
Anthracothorax dominicus [N]	Antillean Mango
Mellisuga minima [N]	Vervain Hummingbird
Temnotrogon roseigaster [NE]	Hispaniolan Trogon
Ceryle alcyon [M]	Belted Kingfisher
Todus angustirostris [NE]	Narrow-billed Tody
Todus subulatus [NE]	Broad-billed Tody
Nesoctites micromegas [NE]	Antillean Piculet
Melanerpes striatus [NE]	Hispaniolan Woodpecker
Sphyrapicus varius [M]	Yellow-bellied Sapsucker
Tyrannus dominicensis [N]	Gray Kingbird
Tyrannus caudifasciatus [N]	Loggerhead Kingbird
Myiarchus stolidus [N]	Stolid Flycatcher
Contopus caribaeus [N]	Greater Antillean Pewee
Elaenia fallax [N]	Greater Antillean Elaenia
Kalochelidon euchrysea [N]	Golden Swallow
Iridoprocne bicolor [M]	Tree Swallow
Progne dominicensis [N]	Caribbean Martin
Ripara ripara [M]	Bank Swallow
Stelgidopteryx ruficollis [M]	Rough-winged Swallow
Petrochelidon pyrrhonota [MR]	Cliff Swallow
Oporornis formosus [M]	Kentucky Warbler
Orporornis agilis [M]	Connecticut Warbler
Geothlypis trichas [M]	Common Yellowthroat
Microligea palustris [NE]	Ground Warbler
Xenoligea montana [NE]	White-winged Warbler
Wilsonia citrina [M]	Hooded Warbler
Setophaga ruticilla [M]	American Redstart
Coereba flaveola [N]	Bananaquit
Euphonia musica [N]	Blue-hooded Euphonia
Spindalis zena [N]	Stripe-headed Tanager
Piranaga ruba [MR]	Summer Tanager
Phaenicophilus palmarum [NE]	Black-crowned Palm Tanager
Calyptophilus frugivorus neibae [NE]	Chat Tanager (Cordillera Central)
Calyptophilus f. tertius [NE]	Chat Tanager (Sierra Bahoruco)

Molothrus bonariensis [NI]	Glossy Cowbird
Quiscalus niger [N]	Greater Antillean Grackle
Icterus dominicensis [N]	Black-cowled Oriole
Icterus galbula [M]	Baltimore Oriole
Passer domesticus [NI]	House Sparrow
Ploceus cucullatus [NI]	Village Weaver
Lonchura punctulata [NI]	Spice Finch
Lonchura malacca [NI]	Chestnut Mannikin
Carduelis dominicensis [NE]	Antillean Siskin
Loxia leucoptera megaplaga [NE]	White-winged Crossbill
Loxigilla violacea [N]	Greater Antillean Bullfinch
Tiaris olivacea [N]	Yellow-faced Grassquit
Tiaris bicolor [N]	Black-faced Grassquit
Pheucticus ludovicianus [M]	Rose-breasted Grosbeak
Guiraca caerulea [M]	Blue Grosbeak
Passerina cyanea [M]	Indigo Bunting
Ammodramus savannarum [N]	Grasshopper Sparrow
Zonotrichia capensis [N]	Rufous-collared Sparrow